LIVING IN
God's Rhyme

TIM CARTER

LIVING IN GOD'S RHYME

This book is written to provide information and motivation to readers. Its purpose is not to render any type of psychological, legal, or professional advice of any kind. The content is the sole opinion and expression of the author, and not necessarily that of the publisher.

Copyright © 2018 by Tim Carter

All rights reserved. No part of this book may be reproduced, transmitted, or distributed in any form by any means, including, but not limited to, recording, photocopying, or taking screenshots of parts of the book, without prior written permission from the author or the publisher. Brief quotations for noncommercial purposes, such as book reviews, permitted by Fair Use of the U.S. Copyright Law, are allowed without written permissions, as long as such quotations do not cause damage to the book's commercial value. For permissions, write to the publisher, whose address is stated below.

Note that scripture verses were taken from The New International Version Bible, used by permission

Printed in the United States of America.

ISBN 978-1-949746-56-3   (Paperback)
ISBN 978-1-949746-57-0   (Digital)

Lettra Press books may be ordered through booksellers or by contacting:

Lettra Press LLC
18229 E 52nd Ave.
Denver City, CO 80249
1 303 586 1431 | info@lettrapress.com
www.lettrapress.com

Contents

Chapter 1, A Story
  The Suicide I Hide 3

Chapter 2, The First of Days
  Faith Without Trust 11
  The Lamb of God 14
  His Spoken Word 16
  What Does God Want Me to Tell You 18
  Thoughts from the Index Card Box 21
  My High Tide 25
  Nothing Greater 26
  Monday Morning the Night Before 29
  Pens, Pencils and Crayons 31
  The Rhyme of God, the Rhyme of Me 34
  Do We Do This to Jesus? 37
  An Introvert's Voice 39
  The Love God Gives 41
  Yes or No, Matthew: 10:32-33 44
  Have We Seen, Have We Heard, Are We Healed 47
  One Day in the World 50
  Matthew 14:13-21 52
  Sudden Day 53
  The Prisoner 55
  Another Day Today 58
  If You Don't Mind, I Don't 60
  His Word May It Lead Us 63
  The Missionary's Mission 65
  2 Timothy 4:2 68
  Thoughts from a Writer of Words 70
  The Healing in Forgiveness 72
  One Thought Became Another 75

The Writer of Words 77
What Have We Learned? 79
I Will Not Write of This 81
My Changing Prayer 83
The Story of My Prayer 85
Random Thoughts from a Green Paper Napkin Holder 87
The Dinner Table 89
No Title, I know Not the Words 91
There Is Only One Rhyme That Will Last Beyond Time 93

Chapter Three, Taken From the Attic
Poems About You 99
For My Wife 100
Still untitled after all these years 101
Homeward September 102
Page 96, still untitled 103
Moments of Bridges 104
Ships & Lakes & Me 105

Chapter Four: The End of The Days for Writing a Book
This One Scares Me 109
The Prophets of Yesterday, Are They Heard Today? 111
Is This The Human Condition (This is not a question) 114
As Only You Can 116
Corners 117
For Those He Loves 119
Draw Me Closer 122
Meet Me 123
The Gentleness of Faith 125
Talk Around the Table 127
Days of Discouragement 129
A Writer's Confession 131
An Eternal Heart 135
Inspired By Babies 137
The Veil Torn, the Presence of God 140
Thoughts from Reading Peter 142

Chef Shell's 143
The Daily Eclipse 145
Do Not Let Me Sit 147
Whose Words 149
I Have Nothing 151
Thoughts on the Way to Church 152
The Book on the Shelf 153
Another Day 155
Yesterday Today and Tomorrowday 157
Meaningless Words 159
What Have I Done for You? 162
Drinking After Ten 164
Labor Days 166
The Next Step of Promises 168
Pray Always 170
Like My Father 172
Amazing 174
Of Truth and Lies 176
Words That Are Shared 177
Matthew 16:6 179
The Wonder of God's Way 182

Chapter 5, Drawing on Her Inspiration
Introduction - Tim 187
Hello Readers 188
A Soldier for the Lord 191
Be a Soldier Unto the Lord 193
The Reflection 197
Protected Forever and Ever 199
An Unplanned Pregnancy 203
Whichever Way the Wind Will Blow 207

Chapter Six, The End of the Story
A September to Remember 211
Concluding Prayer 213

To my wife Mary Lou,
whose support throughout our
44 years of marriage has been one of
God's Rhymes in my life.

If you give
Him the times,
as you live
His word rhymes

Introduction

God puts people in your life to lead you where you may not have thought you would or wanted to go. The Marketing Coordinator I was working with on God Still Rhymes said that I needed to have a book page on Facebook. For God's Rhyme I posted a few of the poems from the book and dates of book signing events on my personal Facebook page. I was not big on Facebook and wasn't completely comfortable with using it to promote the book. I was on the wrong end of the discussion and agreed to start a Facebook page for the books. And, I was told that I needed to post daily.

There was one problem. I didn't know what to do with the page after setting it up. How could I get people interested in looking at the page and be interested in what I had to say day after day. After about a week of floundering around an idea came to me, "Write the next book on Facebook." That sounded better than anything else I could think of.

With a few exceptions that are noted in the book, the poems were written and posted on the God Still Rhymes Facebook page. I was able to write and post seventy two new poems in seventy seven days. There were good days and ok days and absolutely amazing days. As a business page the number of views are noted. In addition to the poems some of the thoughts that went into the idea and writing of the poems follow.

The last chapter contains poems I wrote that were inspired by drawings by the daughter of a friend. Gwen Allen is a very talented young woman. A senior in high school, she was inspired to draw some pictures while attending a women's retreat at her church. I believe they need to be shared. I found hope in her drawings.

I have been blessed by writing the poems in this book. I found that most of the ideas came from my Bible reading. That is explained in the reflections at the end of some of these poems. This book has been an experience in growth in my relationship with God, and my desire to walk with God daily, and the need to be constantly thankful to God for his blessings in my life.

Tim Carter,
Washington DC, October 15, 2017

Chapter 1, A Story

The Suicide I Hide

Introduction

This is the story I was asked to tell,
The story of one, a man, who fell,
Who fell in his own eyes,
Who fell from a life of lies.
There were those days that he lied.
Other days he tried to hide
So no one would find
What was in his mind.

Chapter One, In the Beginning

Growing up in the world shy
He was able to get by,
Though he rarely felt rejection
He so often felt a sense of dejection.

Maybe it came from their need to protect him,
Of parents who still worried about the urgency
That at his birth had required immediate surgery,
Wanting to protect the doctor's correction.

He thought he knew, though was never sure,
Only knowing that their love was pure.
Physically, surgically he was healed
But emotionally his lips were sealed.

He just never learned to speak,
He had just become so meek.
Meek, though certainly he was not always mild.
No, he was not always that mild mannered child.

Chapter Two, Growing

As he grew older
He became bolder.
Though there were still times that he withdrew
From life, though it was only a few.

Yes, he got through school,
He was nobody's fool.
He thought that his life he understood.
He knew bad and he hoped for the good.

In his work he did well,
He had some skills to sell.
He moved up, never down,
He moved – yes, at times down.

Chapter Three, Disheleved Rhymes

He married the love of his life.
She helped relieve some of the strife.
You see, there were still demons
He hid until he shared the reasons.

There are some things learned in youth,
That even knowing they are wrong,
Stay with you forever, for so long
You hide, knowing you lied to those you love.

There was no abuse,
No one to accuse,
Just a wrong
Lasting too long.

With the love of his wife
They added a family to their life.
Both were involved as they grew.
It was a family everyone knew.

Looking back he knew
That growing inside
Was a tumor that grew,
The ugly sin of pride.

Pride began to tear at the joy he knew
When early in the marriage he came to know Jesus,
The saving grace of the father through his Son.
Then one day he forgot what Jesus had done.

Pride, an ugly word,
A word that eats at your soul
And feeds you with lies
About who you are.
Pride led him where he knew he should not go.
It led him from the truth of his life
Into the shadows of spiritual death,
A double life without meaning.

In the name of religion,
In the name of his employer,
In the name of his family,
In the name of his wife,
Profane without shame
He continued to play a game,
A game without a winner
Leaving only a sinner.

He was good at his job,
He thought he was one with God,
Though in his heart he knew he wasn't,
Not when he would dare
To try to have an affair.
That became the ultimate in pride.
When the rhymes left
And the lies continued
He knew he was lost
And knew there was a cost
To be paid
For the life he had made,
Not just for him,
But for so many others.

Chapter Four, Far From Home

He had to take a job farther from home.
That is when his world began to collapse.
Everything had been taken, not given,
Because of his sin, his distance from God.

Pride had taken all he had
And turned it into regret and revulsion,
Revulsion with himself and the life he had made
For not just him, but for his family.

Leaving work one day he could take no more.
He knew what he wanted and what he did not.
As his family left for a night of fun
He settled in bed with every pill he could find.

The next morning his wife realized
That pride had lost, had not taken this one.
The man she loved was saved, not once,
But twice by God, on the cross and in that room.

Chapter Five, Those Almost Left Behind

Seeing his family gathered in a hospital room
He wished he could sweep if he could find a broom.
He wished the past could be swept
To a place where no one wept.

Worse than the living with his pride
Was the pain of those at his side,
The looks of hurt, of crying in the dirt
And the wondering why he wanted to die.

All he had known was the pain
Of a life living in constant rain,
A pain he now saw in the faces
That belonged in much better places.

How do you tell a child it wasn't her fault,
How do you ask your wife to forget the hurt
You have caused to those you love,
How do you explain the choice of death over life?

You see that their pain is greater
Than on that day when you left work.

Chapter Six, Redemption

God has a plan and we make choices,
Quietly sometimes without voices,
Without voicing to others, those we love, our needs,
Or hearing the voice of God who knows our needs.

It was in the aftermath of recovery
God began his work of restoration.
It was a work in the man of rediscovery,
Of the love God had for his situation.

As the man opened his heart
He could feel the healing start
As it surged throughout his soul
He now knew that was God's goal.

It has been years
With fewer tears,
Without the fears
As he draws near
To the love of God,
For the plan
That was always there,
For the love and care
That God does share
As the sinner repents
For the time ill spent.

Concluding Chapter

The man who talked to me,
Who gave me word after word
So his story could be heard,
That man you know is me.

Thank you Lord for your patience,
Thank you Lord for your love,
Thank you Lord for your Son,
Thank you Lord for saving me.

Chapter 2, The First of Days

Faith Without Trust

As I look back at the miles,
Seeing the tears and the smiles,
Having stirred up so much dust,
Why did I think that I must?

I do believe all that you have for me
And I know that who I am you see,
That you have plans for what I should be,
That you want us to be we.

To one father Jesus asked if he believed,
Believed that his child would be healed and live.
To which the man replied, I believe,
Help me overcome my unbelief.

I don't know about you,
But that is me.

I have faith that God's word is true,
That his promises are real.
He has changed me, I am made anew.
I have on my heart his seal.

But there are times I feel left out,
When I have doubt
About what he has planned,
About where with him I stand.

I sometimes wander about.

My faith, what is it
As I try to make it fit
Into the ways of the world
As at night I lay curled,

Curled up in a ball
Waiting for his call.

On one of my good days
We had a talk, God and me.
I had taken the time
To read of his ways.

I know he was pleased
That I had taken the time
And in that time it was me,
It was me that he seized.

He told me that my faith,
Though ever growing,
Would never be what it could
If I didn't trust.

I need to trust when I am fearful,
I need to trust when I am tearful,
I need to trust in the good times
And when there are no rhymes.

If I truly accept the death of his Son
For my salvation, my redemption,
For his promise of eternity,
Then I need to not just believe.

I need to trust that he
Is in control always,
And in all ways,
No matter what I see.

He loves me,
He blesses me,
And as my trust in
His promises,
His word grows,
My faith will also.

The Lamb of God

*Do not weep! See, the Lion of the tribe of Judah,
the root of David, has triumphed. He is able to open
the scroll and its seven seals."
Then I saw a Lamb, looking as if it had been slain,
standing at the center of the throne . . .
Revelation 5:5-6*

As I sat reading of John's vision
I felt as if I never fully understood
That for eternity God's decision
Remains forever for my good.

Yes, I have read of the cruelty
Of his beating on the way to the cross,
Of the agony of his death,
The death of God's son.

The death of my condemnation.

I know that by God's grace
I will be with him forever.
I know I will see his face
And feel his loving embrace.

But reading the words of what John saw,
Though they shouldn't, they rub my wounds raw:
A Lamb, looking as if it had been slain,
Knowing it is from my pain.
The resurrected Jesus in human form
Appeared as if he had been reborn,
Perfect in every way.
And with us he will stay.

Though forgiven, the wounds I caused
Are still there, showing his care.
May I never forget his love for me,
The suffering,
So that with him I will forever be.

Reflection on The Lamb of God

In God's Rhyme I wrote a poem called "Love" about the pain and suffering Jesus experienced on the way to and on the cross. (Read "The Case for Christ" by Lee Stroebel) When I read the line in Revelation it inspired this poem, I was struck by the Lamb looking like it had been slain. I know that my sins have been forgiven. I know that my sins and my straying cause God pain, but I never really thought about how deeply that must affect God. And then it is ever harder to grasp how much he loves me if the scars are still visible.

His Spoken Word

In the beginning

How powerful is God's word?
His word is spoken to us
Through the scriptures,
Through answered prayer,
Through communion with him,
In the quiet and the confusion.
His word is Holy for He is Holy.

How powerful is God's word?
Through his word the Heavens
And the earth, the universe,
Were spoken into existence.

That being so, his word can shape
And mold these earthen vessels of clay
Into sons and daughters
Who will inherit joy everlasting.

Today

By the Word that created all
He has seen his creation fall,
Yet he sent the Word, his Son,
To speak the words, "*It is done.*"

For him, a thousand years is as a day,
As a day is as a thousand years.
Has it been only days in his time
That we have been living in fear?

We have caused the pain,
We have caused the strain
That has left a stain
Even as it does rain.

But as always through his word
He speaks to us in words of love.
But our vision has been blurred
Because we do not look above.

Yes, we have shut the doors,
Doors to our sins, to our souls,
When we should be opening the door
And inviting God and his word into our lives.

If you haven't, please do it today.
The fragrance of salvation, a gentle breeze
That refreshes us through the open door.
The open door, the only way.

May God heal your pain, your suffering, your fears.
May you let Him heal your soul for eternity.

Reflection on His Spoken Word

On the drive home from work one day I thought of writing about pain, the pain that so many of us have gone through and are going through today. It was going to be written with someone in mind. When I got home, I got out my Study Bible and started looking up verses about pain and then sorrow. None seemed to fit the emotion I wanted to write about. Then there was that gentle hand again guiding me. I found a small piece of notebook paper marking the first page of John's Gospel. On it was the beginning of a poem I had written a couple of years ago.

Prayer and the answer!

What Does God Want Me to Tell You

No, that is not a question, it is his will.
I can speak nothing into existence,
But his word will not let me be still.
From me he has taken my resistance.

So I pray,
What do I say?

All he says is pray,
I'll lead the way.
I will not lead you astray
In the prayers you will say.

Dear Father in Heaven who sacrificed for me,
Sacrificed your Son so that I, that we, could see
All of your love, all of your glory for eternity.
Believe, be baptized, with you we will be.

Dear Lord, I thank you for your mercy
In the life I live.
I thank you that all I can be
Is what you give.

Today Lord I pray,
I pray for those who do not know you,
For those who have not heard your word,
For those who have been led astray
From the Truth, the Life and your Way.
I pray that all of your sons and daughters
Will rely on your strength,
That I will surrender my will
And live with the strength of your grace;

For this I pray for everyone.
Lord I pray for those
Without the basics of life,
Food, water and shelter;
For orphans and widows
As you have commanded us;
For those who struggle with
Addictions, and those who feed the addictions;
For those who are abused and their abusers;
For those who are bullied and the bullies;
For those in prison,
In hospitals,
Those who are lost,
Runaways,
Those who have been kidnapped
And their kidnappers,
Those with mental illnesses,
Those who hate,
Terrorists,
Those living under oppression,
For persecuted Christians
In the Middle East,
Especially Coptic Christians
Living under daily
Persecution.
I pray Lord for
Those who are sick,
Those with terminal illnesses,
For the health and salvation
Of family and friends.
And Lord, I pray for
Our country,
I pray that we repent
From our sins against you
And allow you into our
Daily lives, no matter where we are,

Finally Lord
I thank you for loving me
For helping me to see
What I should be
When we are we.

Forgive me for my sins,
Keep me from temptation.
But most of all Lord
I ask that you help me
To accept your Holy Spirit
Dwelling within me,
Help me to allow your strength
To be my guide
To show me the answers.

Help me Lord,
Help us all
To answer your call
That after baptism
We go out and spread
The Gospel.

For this I pray in the name of Jesus.
Amen and amen again.

Thoughts from the Index Card Box

"Here I am! I stand at the door and knock.
If anyone hears my voice and opens the door
I will come out and eat with that person,
and they with me." Rev 4:19

Jesus, he is here,
Here, there and everywhere.
We do not always see him
Because we have shut the door.
So he knocks and calls our name
So we may hear his voice and open the door.

He seeks us out
As in our lives we move about,
Here, there,
There and everywhere.

It is the door to our heart
That he wants to enter through
So we may have a new start
To the lives we are living through.

We will sit at his table
And be more than able
To do more than before
We opened the door.

Christ redeemed us from the curse of the law
by becoming a curse for us. Gal 3:13

His creation falling, sinning
Against God and his Law,
Commandments we would not keep.
Only occasionally forgiveness did we seek.

But God so loved us,
So wanted us to be with him,
That he sent his Son Jesus,
To be sacrificed for our sin.

Accepting and believing
In the final atonement,
His sacrifice on the cross
Redeems us from our loss.

God cursed himself
Through his Godly Son,
A curse we deserved
But now "it is done."

"For my Father's will is that everyone that looks to the Son and believes in him shall have eternal life, and I will raise them up on the last day." John 6:40

Raised up on the last day,
For what more could we pray.
But for now on this earth we stay
Merely earthen vessels of clay.

But through God's grace
And our undying faith
These earthen vessels of clay
Will be made anew one day.

We have been made righteous in his sight,
Redeemed in his eyes,
Our sins forgiven,
And through our love for him
We will live in his glory.
Starting with the Christmas story
We are now with God made right.

*"If anyone hears my words but does not keep them,
I do not judge that person. For I did not come to
judge the world, but to save the world.
There is a judge for the one that rejects me and does not
accept my words; the very words that I have spoken
will condemn them at the last day." John 12: 47-48*

Do we worry when we're in no hurry?
As we live our lives do we give
Even a thought to what we ought
To be praying instead of saying?

He's knocking at the door,
Open it before it is too late.
There is so very much more
If you consider your fate.

And we who will not be rejected
Must spread the word
So that those living dejected
Will hear God's saving Word.

*"To the person who is victorious I will give them
the right to sit with me on my throne, just as I
was victorious and sat down with my Father on his throne."
Rev: 3:21*

Reflection on Thoughts from the Index Card Box

Sometimes I have a good day at work. Today was one of those because I had an idea for today's write. A few years ago I started to write down notes on index cards of Bible verses or thoughts I had while reading. They have sat for a few years not collecting dust because they have been stored in a box. I have found that things stored in my brain get lost. So this idea came to me (you figure out from where) to put a few of the notes into one poem. This is the result of safe storage and God's answer to prayer.

My High Tide

My life is
like the ocean,
With highs and lows
And an ever ebbing flow
From your love into the deep.

You, Lord, are my high tide,
Covering my fears, the tears I cry
As I face each and every day
Knowing it is you I must obey.

Unable to count the grains of sand
In this life I live.
It is with your love I can stand
By the love you give.

Your love covers my transgression,
And the world's aggression,
That as it seeks me out
It no longer has clout.

For me there is no longer any harm.
I am embraced by your loving arms.
Living in your grace
I can finish the race.

Yes, at low tide living in this world
Where thoughts and deeds are just swirled,
Swirled around with too much sound,
Now in your high tide your peace I have found.

Nothing Greater

Jesus loves me this I know,
As children we all have heard,
Because the Bible tells me so.
These words we did sing
As church bells did ring.

We also know that we are told
To live our lives in a way that is bold.
As the children of God in Heaven above
We are to share with others his love.

To share we must accept what he is giving
And show his love in the way we are living.
We must not just love him, but love him enough
To share his love even when the times are tough.

And they will be.
Will we?
When we decide,
Will there be pride?
Is it our love
Or the love of God?

Our love for God should show his holiness,
And never be a reflection of our loneliness.
A love that is true,
Though with many shaded hues
Should always be a reflection
Of God and his perfection.

As we share his love are we perfection?
Salvation has made us righteous in his sight,
So as we meet him in eternity we are a reflection
Of who he is, of his love, of his power and his might.

But on this earth as we proclaim his word
To those who are lost and have not heard,
The love we give to others that shows our care,
It is the love of God that he has for us that we share.

Yes, we love our sisters and brothers,
Love them more than enough to share,
To share his love for us with others
That broken as we are he will always care.

This love we share
Must come from God.
For our love alone,
The love of man,
Never will have the power
Of the Almighty
God who loves.
His love is perfect,
It is righteous,
It is forgiveness,
His love is Holy.

Our love will reflect the love of God.
And though we are a reflection of him,
In our humanness we live in sin,
Sin that his Son has overcome.

We are not God,
We never will be.
But as his children
We have been reborn,
And now can show the way
To the one and only truth
And through his love eternal life.

Reflection on Nothing Greater

My wife and I went to a double belated birthday get together and 4th of July party. The couple are a good Christian couple. It is obvious that God has worked in their lives and in their business. It is always encouraging to hear people talk about God's timing in their lives, how the answer to prayer sometimes comes at unexpected times and unexpected ways. The following idea unexpectedly came to mind on the drive home.

This poem took longer to write than I thought it would. I had the idea that our love is not as great as God's love. How can it be? We are not perfect on this earth. I knew part way through writing that I was trying to write the poem I wanted. I wanted to go deeper into the difference of our love and God's love. I was getting stuck in the middle of sentences and stanzas and rhymes. When I gave in and followed the words he wanted me to write, it was quickly finished. His love is patient!
Thank you Lord.

Monday Morning the Night Before

There is nothing to say
Nothing new in any way
Except the thunder I hear
Slowly as it moves near

There is one difference I have noticed
Since putting letters together that form the words
Well now two
I have misplaced the punctuation
And one line is too long

But through it all,
On this day I still hear
His voice, his call.
He is still, as always, here.

Always and forever
Includes tomorrow,
Knowing the he will never
Leave me in my sorrow.

Another day to be in his presence
Another hour to be thankful
That through his grace my penance,
He has taken from me, it is paid in full.

So, I will awake in the morning,
To the rising Son.
There will be no mourning,
The battle he has won.

The only fear I will know
Is the awesome reverence
That by his holiness I must show
To God for taking my repentance.

Monday morning's prayer is
That all my desires
Are that I live wanting what is his,
His love for me is all I desire.

Pens, Pencils and Crayons

We hear God's word spoken,
The Scriptures read aloud
To those who are broken,
Who mingle among the crowd.

We who have aged with time
Are like a pen in the hand
Of a scribe writing a line
In a gentle sea of sand.

We have written our lines
Of our many times,
Of the many dimes
We have spent on fines.

We have lived and written our lines
Of our past, the good and the bad.
Hopefully they include a line or two
Of the blessings we have had.

And there is the pencil used in school
As those who are younger
Write lines of times in the future,
Lines of unknown times.

With eraser in hand they can wipe away
Imagined futures and never lived pasts.
They can boldly write with nothing to say
Unless we show them the way that lasts.

Ever evolving, the developing mind
Will, as the search continues, find
The wrong or right way to write
The lines of tomorrow's insight.

(Their future before them,
Formed by the writings
Of yesterday, asking them
What demons they are fighting.)

The crayon of the child,
One color in a box
Of many hued colors
That has no lock.

Pictures of smiles,
Squiggly lines,
Colors outside,
Some inside.
They are eager to learn,
We love them as they are,
It is nothing to earn.
They shine like the evening star.

(They come to us with open hearts,
Knowing we love them for who they are.
And as each and every new day starts
They have no fear of what the colors are.)

Someone sees
Innocence,
Acceptance,
Trust,

Curiosity
Beauty
And love
Spread around
The room,
No longer in a box.

Don't make God complicated.
Jesus made it simple.

And he said: "Truly I tell you, unless you
Change and become like little children,
You will never enter the kingdom of heaven."
Matthew 18:3

The Rhyme of God, the Rhyme of Me

There may be no rhymes
As in other times.
But it is not that the Lord
Has struck a lost chord.
(if he did it would be sung
as every church bell was rung)
His rhyme is his word,
The scriptures we read
Through which he plants the seed,
With hope that we have heard.

It is through his grace
That we see his face
In those we meet
And those we greet.

If we believe,
In us lives his rhyme
Forever in time.
He will not deceive.

Then I decided to write
About something right,
But got it wrong
Because it was me,
Me, just me, alone.

I can wander in this world,
Oblivious to all that is good.
I can try by myself
To lift myself up,

Up above the
Hustle without
The bustle,
And fail
Because the bustle
Of this world
Is the hustle
That tells me
All I see
Is all I need.

Then I awake from what I hope was a dream,
Hoping that all is not what it seemed.
I look in the mirror and see
The reflection of what I used to be,

What I used to be before
My Savior redeemed me,
Made me righteous in his eyes,
The eyes of his Father in Heaven above.
Every moment of every day I felt his love.
A love for me and those who surround
My life, who have oft times run aground.

I pray that what I dream
Is never real.
I pray that what may seem
Somewhat surreal
Is nothing more than a bad dream
From a bad movie scene.

As I live I pray that temptation
I turn over to my Savior
Who has conquered my sin
No matter where I've been.

When I turn my back
I lose my sight
Of what is wrong
And who is right.

May I focus my eyes,
The eyes of my soul,
So that to my sin I die.
He has mended the hole.

Reflection on The Rhyme of God, the Rhyme of Me

Someone once asked me at a book signing where the name God's Rhyme came from for the first book. From Him I said, He is the Rhyme. Later I realized that I also had a poem in the book with that title. What a memory!

Do We Do This to Jesus?

Do you believe that every word Jesus spoke is true,
Or do you believe of all the words in just a few;
His word at creation,
His word of the resurrection,
His word of the door,
The bread of life,
His Father in Heaven,
His word over death,
His word that heals?
Yesterday,
Today and
Tomorrow,
It is his word we must follow.

And then we are told,
What so ever you do
To the least of my brothers,
That you do unto me.

Do we as Christians mistreat Jesus?
Do we see him in those we meet,
Those we pass in the street,
The homeless one,
The child on the run,
The one in rags,
Possessions in bags?

Are we better than them?
Are they not a reflection of,
A reflection of his love?
And when we judge them to be less,
Can we expect to be blessed?

Jesus ate with sinners,
And those less fortunate
In the eyes of the world.
Must we ask ourselves why?
Do we ever try,
Try to understand
His word is a command?

I can hurt Jesus when alone,
With no one else, just my bones.
But I must not mistreat him,
Must not commit the sin
Of judging him
When I do others.

Reflection on Do We Do This to Jesus?

We may never know, perhaps the one we judge to be less is the one God sent to bring us to Him.

Later in the day after writing this poem I was reading the Beatitudes in Matthew 5-7. This poem is me. I found myself being spoken to in the words of Jesus in the Sermon on the Mount. And I was reminded in Chapter 7 of this, *"Do not judge or you too will be judged. For in the same way you judge others, you will be judged, and with the measure you use, it will be measured to you."* Forgive me Lord. Always keep me mindful of the plank in my eye.

An Introvert's Voice

It is that voice inside,
Inside his brain, his mind,
That is like a moving train.
Silently, it is that kind.

Thoughts like the wind,
Blowing brain matter around,
Scattering rhyming letters
Everywhere without a sound.

It's not that he has nothing to say,
And it's not that he has lost his way.
It's more like he has turned to stone
From feeling safe when being alone.

He can smile
For a while.
Yes, he can talk,
But would rather walk.

I guess it's hard to explain
This silent running train.
Thoughts are there having formed words,
So many words that no one has heard,

Words that haven't found a voice,
Unsure of how to make a choice.
For him, uncertain,
He closes the curtain.

Unable to explain,
His voice is quiet.
So he writes
Words of rights,
Words of wrongs.
It is here
Where he is strong
So you can hear.

An unspoken after thought:
Not sure it makes any sense.
More an exercise in
Rhyming introspection
Than an explanation.
Or maybe it is more.

The Love God Gives

On his head thorns for a crown,
The thorns of my transgression.
Because he loved me I bow down
And profess to him my confession.

An all knowing God who created all we know,
Knowing the good and bad seeds we would sow
Still breathed into each one of us life,
Knowing that he one day pay would the price.

I wonder as I write these stanzas of words
Why, if he knew we would become a herd
Of wandering sheep,
His word he still keeps.

Though he knew our sin, our wandering ways
His love never wanders, the same it stays.
Yes, he is a just God who will punish
The unrepentant who refuse to believe.

But his love is always there
When we are ready to share,
To share in his reign,
That removes our shame.

He is a just God,
A righteous God,
He is a God of love,
He is a God of glory.

The Holy love of God
Forgives, it gives
Hope and blessing,
Joy in our sadness,
It lifts us up
As we share the cup,
The blood of his covenant
With the lost remnant.

From us he deserves
Our constant praise
As he preserves
Our living days.

And sometimes I wonder
Why he gave us free will
Knowing we would wander,
Knowing he would love us still.

His ways are not our ways.
Thankfully we should pray
A prayer of thanksgiving
That with him we are living.

Knowing all, who would hear his call,
He prepared for those who believe
That he alone is Holy in Glory,
A promise at the end of the story.

It is a story of his love,
The pain of his love,
The magnitude of his love,
The forgiveness of his love,
And the hope of his love.

He sent Jesus to deliver the message,
To pay the price to make us right,
To show the way, to open the door
That we may forever live in his sight.

Thank you, Lord
For your love for me,
Your love for my neighbor.
Thank you, Lord,
Thank you for eternity.

Yes or No, Matthew: 10:32-33

"Whoever acknowledges me before others,
I will also acknowledge before my Father in Heaven.
But whoever disowns me before others,
I will disown before my Father in Heaven."

Words Jesus spoke as he sent out the twelve
To spread the Word, to heal the sick, raise the dead
And drive out impure spirits, these words he said.
They were given authority each one of the twelve.

Instructions were given regarding those who did believe
And those among God's chosen who would not receive.
I will acknowledge and I will disown,
Either way the seeds will be sown.

All of this makes me wonder, no I know
That I can no longer take the easy path.
I must help plant seeds that will grow,
Watered by grace, avoiding God's wrath.

I must remember that I do not do this alone,
That if I, and I do, get weary to the bone,
That through his strength alone
My heart, my soul he does hone.

I must tell the truth, like it or not,
That there is only one way.
No, there are two words you can say,
Yes or no, that's all that you've got.

I once wrote these lines,
Heaven or hell,
what will it be
before the
Judgement throne?

The easy road is to spread the glory.
But the true road includes the full story.
It is ours to decide
As we face the divide,

Do we love our brothers and sisters
Enough to tell them the truth
That there will be resisters,
Those who will bear bad fruit?

But without our telling them of the choice,
The love or the wrath for eternity,
We are guilty of denying them the choice
Of preventing, avoiding God's enmity.

The good news is all of the news,
Leading the lost to a new way.

An explanation of what lead me to writing at this point in the book.

I never cease to be amazed where prayer leads me. My Bible reading lately has not been as consistent as it should be. But I have found more often than not when I asked God to direct me what to read it is all over the place. There is no continuity in where I am led. But there has been one thing that has been constant. I stop reading when I come to the point He wants to make. Then I make note of it or if I am fortunate I put His words into a written poem. This happened tonight, July 17, 2017.

Reflection on Yes or No, Matthew: 10:32-33

I have been wondering what direction this book was going to take. I believe the direction in which I am being led is to not just write of God's love, but of His full plan for eternity. He loves us all, He wants us to be with Him. But after hearing His complete word, the decision is ours. His love does not require that we follow Him blindly, we have been given free will to accept or reject our adoption as sons and daughters of the Holy God of all that is good. He wants our love because we truly love Him. And He has given us the way to live in his love.

I make no apologies for speaking His word. My life will be better and I pray that everyone who reads this will have a better life also.

Have We Seen, Have We Heard, Are We Healed

"*Though seeing, they do not see,
though hearing they do not hear or
understand.
In them is fulfilled the prophecy of Isaiah;
You will be ever hearing but never
understanding;
you will be ever seeing but never perceiving.
For this people's heart has become
calloused;
They hardly hear with their ears,
and they have closed their eyes.
Otherwise they might see with their eyes,
hear with their ears,
understand with their hearts
and turn, and I would heal them,*"
Matthew 13: 13-15

The heart keeps the body alive
Pumping blood through our veins
So in living we might thrive,
We might live without bodily pains.

But when calloused our heart becomes,
We seek wealth
Instead of health.
Our days become totals of our sums.

Our hearing, our sight
Do not hear or see the fight
As we run from the light
Into darkness.

This world has forsaken the light.
Living with our adulterous gods of money and sin,
Never knowing what should be right,
Never knowing that tomorrow we may not win.

We believe that the easy road leads to pleasure
As we follow our heart to find the treasure,
The satisfaction of believing we are good,
Not knowing we never really understood.

Have we heard someone speak
That as mere mortals we are weak?
Has someone ever taken our hand
And lifted us up to stand?

Has anyone asked you to listen, to look
At your yesterdays and todays to see what you took,
To see that we have no gain
For what we cause in a world of pain?

Someone please shout,
Shout the world about
About God's saving grace
As we have we run this race.

Be healed,
Your fate sealed
By believing
And receiving
The Son
Of the one
And only God
Who loves us all.
Please,
Hear His call.

Reflection on Have We Seen, Have We Heard, Are We Healed"

Near the end of God's Rhyme I noticed that the poetry was changing. There was more of the pain we cause God. I should correct that, more of the pain I cause God. It culminated with the last poem I wrote for the book, Broken Hearted. It was about how throughout Old Testament and New Testament history we have broken God's heart. I think the God Still Rhymes has that in it also. In writing the third book I am finding that I am being led to continue that theme, that and the need for God in our lives, so that our hearts will not be broken at the end of our days.

The night I wrote the following poem I started reading Mathew 12:38, The Sign of Jonah. When I got to the end of the end of Chapter 13, verse 15, I stopped. The verses beyond this will bring joy to believers. Hopefully we can lead non-believers past verse 15 and into verse 16 and beyond.

One Day in the World

She has been hurt,
Left in the dirt.
No longer standing on her feet,
She lays crying in her defeat.

Through tear filled eyes
She looks up at the sky
And asks the question, why
Sometimes the winner is the lie.

Oh, she did often try
To look beyond the lie,
But it was always there,
Everyday, everywhere.

Was it a test of her faith
As the tears poured like rain?
Could she feel God's embrace
As he relieved her of pain?

Her prayers, the prayers of others,
That lie after lie God would smother.
Now looking forward, not in a hurry,
Believing what Jesus said, do not worry.

Her future is in God's hands.
Believing she now understands
That without his presence
The world would make no sense.

She will no longer struggle
As the world would demand.
She will pray and wait
And with God will stand.

She will turn to God,
Trust in his word.
And his plan for her, his plan,
That the world has not heard.

Reflection on One Day In the World

I wrote this for someone near and dear to my heart, one of our daughters. It is also for the rest of us that have struggled with hurt and the world around us. Pray that God will bless those hurting and ourselves.

Matthew 14:13-21

After the beheading of John the Baptist, Jesus withdrew to a solitary place. The crowd followed him. Seeing them, he healed the sick. As night approached his disciples told him to send the crowd to the nearby villages to buy themselves food. This was not going to happen. Jesus told the disciples to feed the crowd. With only five loaves and two fish he gave thanks in prayer. The crowd was fed.

Jesus gave thanks and prayed
For the loaves and fish to be multiplied.
The needs of the crowd were satisfied,
He healed them,
He fed them,
Their blessings were multiplied.

Our needs, our prayers the Lord receives
If we have believed,
If we have received,
He blesses the one who believes.

As Jesus prayed
His prayer was answered,
Answered
With abundance.

God answers our prayers,
He answers them with abundance.
Ask what is pleasing to him
And he will pour out his grace
Which is beyond our knowing.
But his abundance,
His love, will always be showing,
Our blessings will be multiplied.

Sudden Day

The first day of the week,
We worship him in church
As comfort in our lives we seek
Before out the doors we lurch.

Tomorrow begins the weak days,
Those days when we can easily forget
What on Sunday he did say.
As we step in the puddles our feet are wet.

It is me
In the mirror
I do see.
In the morning
There is a warning
In the prayer said
That all I need
Is his word to heed
And I will be led
My soul will be fed
And then I open the door
To the world that wants more.
Each and every day I see
A reflection in the mirror.

But there are so many about
As our lives we live out
That have not heard
Us speak of his word.

We must care,
We must share,
Let them know
As we sow
The seeds
That will feed
More than five thousand,
More than loaves and fish,
More than they could ever wish
In years beyond a thousand.

We can lead them to eternity.
Away from God's enmity,
So that when it does arrive
Sudden Day they will survive.

The Prisoner

Locked in a prison having committed a crime.
It has been done over and over throughout time.
If we do harm, there must be punishment,
Not to right our wrongs, but for discouragement,
To let those who may want to do harm
Know that evil should set off an alarm.

Since the fall in the garden
Man and woman lived in sin,
Their hearts they did harden
As away from God they did spin,
Turning their hearts and their eyes
From good all the while knowing why.

From that time until today and beyond
We who were made in his image
Have committed sins for which we are fond.
Not just in the garden, but through every age.

We have become prisoners of the evil ways
We live and desire as we live our days.
Our just punishment from a righteous
God who created us, we will never survive.

But through his loving grace,
His desire that we have a place
With him forever and ever
He said that he will erase
Our sin and will remember never.

Our punishment for our sin against him,
For our disobedience, our lust for wrong,
He has provided the sacrifice to make us strong,
To sing of his amazing grace worshiping him.

He is a loving God, a love we do not understand.
His love will wait until we are ready to stand,
To stand above our past and look to heaven above
To see his glory, to feel the need for his love.

He sent his Son to become one of us,
He sent his Son to die for you and me,
To be the sacrifice to make us right,
He loved us so much he sent us Jesus.

And when by grace we accept his gift,
Our lives, our past, our hopes he does lift
From our earthly ways,
Our desire to stray.
By the world we will be mocked
But our lives will not be rocked,
Jesus is our rock
Throughout the ages.

God is good,
He understood
That we would stray
From the way,
The truth and life,
So he took on our strife.

Reflection on the Prisoner

I was thinking about a friend I haven't seen in a while. I remembered one of our breakfast conversations. He was telling me about a man he knew that had been in prison and had turned his life over to the Lord. Another man he knew was going to prison and he was praying that when this man got out of prison he would be able to connect with the first man and have a chance to move beyond his past. The title came to mind. I left the rest up to Him.

Another Day Today

Not an unusual day,
But I'm glad it's over.
There's not a lot to say
Except the day lost its way
About a third into its hours.
Thankfully it didn't turn sour.
Driving home, seeing the clouds
And thinking, as usual, aloud,
With the threat of rain
There were patches of blue.
There were more than a few.
It made me think of a refrain
From a song
From a time long
Beyond the past,
Time that did not last
But is reborn every day
As to the Lord I pray.

Today when I looked at the sky
I knew there was a reason why,
I finally was glad
For the day I had,
Before I saw the blue,
Before I once more knew
That God is always there,
That he always does care.

When I am otherwise
Occupied with my time,
When I feel the seas rise,
At the end of the day
He always finds a way
To share with me his rhyme.
There is beauty in every day
And at the right time
He shows me the way,
Every day, all of the time.

If You Don't Mind, I Don't

If you don't mind
I'll tell you about my brain,
How it does work
And how it does not.

You see with your eyes,
But I see through the rain
Of thoughts and words,
Ideas without rhyme.

You see, I'm not the kind
Who can turn it off and on,
Contrary to what I have told my wife
All these years, together in our life.

It, my mind, is always asking the whys
Of this and that and so much other.
It never stops, there is no rhyme for work.
(There is no rhyme for a missing line)

Unless it is the responsibility I shirk.
Spell check, thank you.
But at times I'd rather you
Not be turned on.

Remember that I forget
What I do not remember,
Notes written down,
Jotted all around.

Just today I did remember
And did my research.
But I found in my search
That I remembered wrong.

No, no rhyme with song
Or long or wrong or strong.
I just moved forward
Trusting I heard God's word.

The more I desire him,
The more I sing a hymn
The more I hear his voice
In my writing choice.

Choices it should have been.
I guess God has many voices,
Perhaps one for each of us
Who have come from dust.

How do I understand
The things in my mind,
As at the end of the day
My life I unwind?

It is by his grace
In my daily race
That I keep pace,
That I leave a trace
Of his work in me,
That it is him you see

When I write the words
That I have just heard
There are twists and turns
From which I learn.

My mind works better when thinking,
When I can do so without blinking
At the thoughts he gives me
At what through him I can be.

PS
I had a half conceived plan.
Point "A "but no point "be".
Now you may see what can
Be done when it is we.
(Sometimes typos can "be" for a reason.)

His Word May It Lead Us

Matthew, Mark Luke and John,
Paul, Peter, Timothy and Jude,
Books and letters written
To show us the way to God's love,
The love of his sacrifice,
The love of his grace,
The love he has for us,
The human race.

Jesus said,
Believe,
Be baptized
And spread the Gospel.

We should not only pray,
Pray every day,
For those who have not heard
His mighty saving word.
We should speak
So that we reach
Those souls we know
Of the gift we have received
So they will not be deceived.
We need to shout
To the world about
That Jesus saves,
He is what God gave
So the end will be better,
So it will not be bitter.

After Thoughts
As believers we can meet in clusters
So that faith and desire we can muster
That as we leave the room
We do not have a sense of doom
But the faith to share,
Share that we care,
That others hear
What we hold dear
To our hearts
So they may start
To see what they can be
That when with Jesus
They will be free.

The Missionary's Mission

They leave the comfort of home
Where they were raised and grown,
Where seeds of faith were sown,
By those who gave them a home.

With the love for those,
These that God chose
Have a yearning to share
The love of God's care.

Traveling across continents and seas
To spread his word and plant the seeds,
Prayerfully hoping that their good deeds
Will show more how God's grace does please.

Where language is a barrier
His word speaks to all,
No matter the carrier,
More will hear your call.

More will hear your call
Because they, many of them,
Love you and those in need
Of hearing a word,
Of sharing a good deed.

It is God's love that leads the missionary.
It is his call that sends them forth,
That sets the missionary on a course.

He has set their hearts on fire
With a spirit full of desire
To help their sisters and brothers
In a way not done by others.

God will bless
Those who help
More who have less,
Those who reach,
Those who teach
The one or more
Who need help.
He will bless evermore.

Pray for those with a heart,
A desire to live apart
From the comforts of a life,
To live with those in strife.
May their living,
May their giving,
Be the gift,
Give a lift
To the spirit
Of many more adrift,
Perhaps not knowing
That as more do hear it,
The words of works
More will share,
More will care
That it is God's word
More will be sowing.

Reflection on The Missionary's Mission

I got the idea for this poem on my way to work . I had a few good lines that I fortunately remembered to write down when I got to work. However, when I wrote it, I struggled. I'm not sure what that means, if anything. Maybe it was because I was writing about something I know little about. But upon reflection during the day I realized that we are all called to be missionaries. Where ever we are we are to share the good news of salvation. At work, on the street, with friends, and especially at home. And it all starts with our story.

2 Timothy 4:2

*Preach the word; be prepared in season and out of season;
correct, rebuke and encourage — with great patience
and careful instruction.*

The word we are to preach,
In and out of season.
This command given to each
Believer for a reason.

We are not all preachers
And certainly not teachers.
But we are all believers
Overcoming deceivers.

If we are to preach the word,
We have to not only read the word,
We have to desire the need
To acknowledge what we read
Is indeed his plan
For a fallen man.

We must hunger for his word,
We must desire to know him,
We must listen to what we have heard,
We must want to do more that sing a hymn.

So we read, we pray,
Asking to understand
What we should say
To obey his command.

Ask God to put in your heart
A desire to live in his embrace
So that you may open a heart
Of someone lost in the race.

If we love God, we will follow him to the ends of the earth.
It is only through him and the sacrifice of his Son,
Through his unending grace that we find our worth.
May we show others the way before the day is done.

Thank you Lord.
Thank you Jesus
For who you are
For all you do.

Thoughts from a Writer of Words

The words I write
I do not speak
Of what is right
Of what we seek

Writing of what we ought to say
Writing words day after day
Words of the truth and the way
Words for what we should pray

And there are those who talk
Who take the time to walk
From the moment of day break
Time for others they do make

And there are those who care
Who speak to God through prayer
That those in need
That he will feed

And there are those who do
The work of God's labor
To help more than a few
Find Jesus their Savior

Through God's power we find
Not just one, but many kind
Though different in how they are used
They spread his word to a world confused

Reflection on Thoughts from a Writer of Words

I thought that I had been led to write about our mission to spread the gospel with the last couple of poems. We are all called spread the Gospel. That starts with our story. It is a personal story that may be easy for others to listen to and engage in talking about your story. Maybe your story will be the start of their story.

The Healing in Forgiveness

*Get rid of all bitterness, rage and anger, brawling
and slander, along with every form of malice.
Be kind and compassionate to one another,
forgiving each other, just as in Christ God forgave you. Eph. 4:30,31*

What needs to be said about this verse?
Though some words may sound terse,
They are covered in the blood
Jesus shed for those he loved.

He has loved
And still does.
Though we have sinned
He has sent a mighty wind
To lift his people up
As we drink from his cup.

We are hurt in so many ways,
Slander, malice, anger and rage.
We are left alone, left defeated.
That's what we do to those God loves.

Sometimes we are they, the other one,
To whom the harm and hurt is done.
We all keep a running total, we tally the sum
Of each and every day they block out the Son.

We are told to forgive throughout God's word,
Told enough that we should have heard,
If with God we live
We are called to forgive.

If God can forgive, so must we.
It is by his forgiving of our sin
That over death we do win.
Why is it so hard for us to see?

God loves so much that he died,
Died in the form of his Son
For the times we lied,
For all we have done.

A death we deserved,
A death we did earn,
But now as we turn
Our place is reserved.

Jesus died once for all,
For all who hear his call,
The call of God's holy grace
That one day we may see his face.
We are but mere mortal man.
How can our sin against another
Be greater than our sin
Against he who created man?

We are commanded to forgive,
So then we must have the trust
To accept the word we have heard
That for God and his children we live.

God loves us
And if we love him,
We will follow his commands.
We will love our neighbor
And with them we will stand.

It is when were are one with God
And one with our fellow man,
Those who have scorned and hurt
That the healing can begin.

God healed us through the death of his Son.
His forgiving of our sins has healed our souls.
Though God is perfect, was he healed of a broken heart?
Does he smile more at each new day's start?

Do We Forget?

It is often said, "I can forgive, but I will never forget."
His word says, our sins forgiven, he will remember no more.
Forgiveness begins the healing, forgetting is the cure.

His ways are not our ways
And our ways are not his ways.
But though we may ask why,
We must always and forever try,
Try to understand
What he commands.

Reflection on The Healing of Forgiveness

The idea for this poem came to me on the afternoon of Day 29 of posting this book's poems on Facebook. Mary Lou and I discussed it at an early dinner at the Atrium Café. After finding the verse I wanted and started walking toward the computer I had this thought; a word smith could spend more than an entire life time writing about God's word, that is how great God is. He is endless. I'm sorry this is so long, but the words kept coming. I never know anymore what He will give me until His voice is quiet. The words He gave me are not the words I was thinking of before I sat down to write.

One Thought Became Another

He who spoke creation into existence
By his word was one with God.
Watching God's creation from Heaven
As man strayed he answered God's call.

Born into his creation he became man.
As one of us he did live
That he might show the way.
To those he loves, his life he did give.

From the beginning he was a blessing
To all of creation, especially man.
Before the beginning, beyond the end
In Jesus we have found more than a friend.

We have found a Savior
Who overcomes our behavior.
This man Jesus as God,
By his life he has saved us.

So we give thanks and praise
For the live God did raise
For the lives Jesus did save
Through the life he gave.

We now have the hope beyond our lives
That it is by God's saving grace we do strive
To honor and praise the Almighty God
And the Savior Son he does love.

Knowing what lies ahead,
Turning from sin to God instead,
Just as Paul did running toward the goal,
So must I with all my heart, all my soul.

An After Thought (from before)

Amazing Grace, I have been found,
When you spoke, I heard the sound.
Now blessings are all around
And your love knows no bounds.

Through grace
You spoke
The blessings
Of your love

Reflection on One Thought Became Another

As I have written before, when I pray for not just direction, but the words, poems do not go where I thought they would. I had the last two lines of this poem come to me at work. On the drive home I thought about writing stanzas of praise and thanks to God. I was going to call it Random Thanks and Praise. I just thought I hadn't written enough praise and thanks into my poems lately. The title of today's poem should tell you what happened.

The Writer of Words

The writer of words of thoughts and dreams,
A never ending stream flowing through his mind,
Sometimes, most times, not knowing what he will find.
In reflection, wondering what it all means.

There is a call that his quiet voice
Will without sound become his choice
To be the messenger of your glory,
Of all the ways only you, God, are holy.

Oh, there are day dreams
And every day schemes
That make his life seem
To be without a rhyme.

There are the times without rhymes,
There is the day with nothing to say.
There are wanderings in his head
That are better left unsaid.

But when he does pray that what he does say,
That what he has heard, is the voice of your word.
Turning everything over to you,
There is nothing he cannot do.

You, Lord, know the readers hearts.
You, Lord, have restored the lost chord.
You, Lord, are there before the day starts.
You, Lord, are above the earthly horde.
So this writer of words does pray

That what you have to say
Will come through to others,
To his sisters and brothers.

The writer needs the reader of his verse
More than the reader has ever known.
It is the reader whose seeds are sown
To help the writer avoid a lifelong curse.

One can write and not share,
That is if one does not care
To follow God's command,
To not drown in the sand.

So the writer writes out of the need
To know that it is God he does heed,
His command to share the gospel
To help make God's children well.

To help make us well not just for a spell.
God's word will our lives save
As we believe in what Jesus gave.
The writer will not drift, accepting God's gift.

Thank you, Lord
For your Word

Reflection on The Writer of Words

I was trying to stay a couple of days ahead in my writingfor Facebook in case I ran into writer's block. But, as happens at times, God has other ideas about writer's block. I had written the previous day's post for Facebook a couple of hours before this one. I had an idea for a poem, then God took over. This is about the soul of a writer who tries to obey when God talks. Now, I just have to listen in the rest of my life.

What Have We Learned?

God's Chosen ones wandered when led.
When they were hungry, they were fed.
Yet so often in their hearts they were dead.
At one time to God they were wed.

Jesus came to save God's people,
Then to save the rest of the nations.
The apostles spread his gospel to God's people,
Paul to the Gentiles of other nations.

We who believe in the saving blood of the Lamb
Are now the children of our Savior's Father.
Our lives have been ransomed from the evil of sin.
We are made righteous in God's sight.

Yet there are times both old and new
Where the words are the same,
But as we live our lives in shame,
In God's eyes there are no rhymes.

His creation, worshiping false idols,
Past and present, not just ignoring God,
But poking him in the eye with poison sticks.
When the good are bad, who does he pick?

Are we born to repeat the failures of Old Testament times?
Have we already in our idolatry crossed too many lines?
If we ignore God are we left to sorrow as our hearts pine
For one, just one of his glorious rhymes

If God is for us, who can be against us?
If we rebel against God, who will protect us?
It is only with God and the blood of Christ
That he can make our lives right.

I am guilty too often in my selfishness.
And when I shut the door
To his eternal and loving forgiveness,
I have less instead of more.

Where is God when we shut the door?
Behind it and out of our lives.

Reflection on What Have We Learned?

This is what I posted with the poem on Facebook.
I finished Facebook posts for day 33 & 34 earlier in the evening. After a few frustrating games of solitaire on my tablet I thought I better get back into reading since my earlier reading was interrupted by the last 2 posts. I was led to read Jeremiah. As I was reading I couldn't help but think that Jeremiah could be talking about America today. I noticed in God Still Rhymes the tone of the poems changed. There was more of a "we need to get right with God" tone. I wasn't sure what the third book would be like. I'm still not sure, but the tone of the last book is still there with more urgency in the tone. I'm not sure where this leads, but I am enjoying the journey.

I Will Not Write of This

On scrolls of old were written words so bold.
Stories were told of hearts with a heavy load
As they strayed and refused to stay,
Stay in the presence of God's holy essence.

Today is another time of giving what is mine,
What weighs me down, what makes my soul drown.
Today I will dedicate my life so I may celebrate
The gift of joy received through God's baby boy.

Today I pray that all that I say,
That all that I do is for you,
Jesus who has saved me so that I might see
Who I am in the great I AM.

You, Lord, are always with me.
My prayer today is that I will be with you,
That with your spirit I am we.
With you, everyday my life you renew.

Why would I ever turn my back
Knowing what the day will lack?
You know, and I do too,
You know and still you love me.

And there, Lord, is your rhyme,
That when I turn away,
You, as you always have, still love me,
That, Lord, for me, is your rhyme.

Lord, take my life and use it as you would,
Help me to be more, than alone, I could.
Help me to do for others all that I should
So they may see that all you have is good.

Not just good, no that is wrong, but great,
If we believe, and trust in you
In all you have done and will do
Because your love for us lifts a weight.

May we never have to hear you say,
*A horrible and shocking thing
has happened in the land:
The prophets prophesy lies,
the priests rule by their own authority,
and my people love it this way.
But what will you do in the end?*
Jeremiah 4:30,31

My Changing Prayer

Lord help me today
As I go on my way,
For this I do pray.

There is more to pray for,
Those who are ill
That their healing will
Also heal their souls.

There are those who need to be found.
Those who have not heard your sound,
There is a world full of pain
Waiting for your healing rain.

And for me, I pray for your help,
What I think I need for myself.
Then I read from Peter's first letter
And know that I need to do better.

Live such good lives among the pagans that,
Though they accuse you of doing wrong,
They may see your good deeds
And glorify God on the day he visits us.
(1 Peter 2:12)

How do I live
With what the life
That surrounds me
Has to give?

I need more than the help for which I ask
If I am to complete my given task.
I must pray for that I understand
That he will carry me across the sand.

So now I pray in a different way.
I ask that God make me aware
That as I go through the day
If I open the door, he is there.

He wants to share his blessings
But I have to open the door
So that I may receive more
Of what he has for me.

I pray that God helps me open my heart
As each new day doe s start.
I pray that I am open to receive
So at the day's end I do not grieve.

Lord, take my life today and use it as you would,
I know that you can do more than I ever could.
I pray that I open the door to allow your spirit
Live within me and that I always hear it.

If I hear you speak
My prayer will be,
It will be complete.

The Story of My Prayer

Dear Father in Heaven I pray that I live for you today.
Dear God I pray that all I say
Is that your will be done, that I live for your Son,
That with the setting sun, your will has been done.

My heartfelt hope, my desire
Is that I not deserve your ire,
That by your indwelling spirit,
The voice of your words, I hear it.

So why today do I feel defeated?
Why do I know there is a distance
Between you and me, and what I see?
Why do I know it is all because of . . .?

As I lay my head upon my bed
I feel the fear that you are not near.
The fear that I know is that of what I did sow,
That when I shut the door, I feel your presence no more.

It is time that is wasted,
In a vast waste land that is my mind.
It is blessings that are squandered
As not trying, you I did not find.

Then your word as I pray to repent:
He has shown you, O mortal, what is good.
And what does the Lord require of you?
To act justly and to love mercy
and to walk humbly with your god.
Micah 6: 8

As I get ready for sleep, as my soul does weep,
I pray that what I did sow, tomorrow will not grow.
As I get ready for sleep, I pray that my soul you keep,
Keep it from the dust, that I do what I must.

Yes, Lord I pray for your help in living my life
In a way that pleases you and those I meet.
I do pray for your help keeping me from strife,
From falling in the gutter of the crowded city street.

But more than that prayer
I pray that you remove the door,
The one that I keep closing,
That when closed keeps you out.

When that door is closed
My voice is silent
And my hearing deaf,
My sight is blinded.

So I ask Lord that this be my prayer:
But, for me, I watch in hope for the LORD,
I wait for God my Savior;
my God will hear me
Micah 7: 7

Random Thoughts from a Green Paper Napkin Holder

How odd our God may seem in the days we dream,
Not odd in the ways we know, nor in what he does, no.
There are times when he gives us his rhymes,
Those occasional times we find that he has opened our mind.

A view from a window,
A word from a friend,
The shape of a shadow,
May it never end.

Out of nowhere we suddenly must share
The rhyme he gave us, as he did with Jesus.
The thought of what we ought,
No, must do because of his trust.

It may be a simple embrace putting a smile on a face
Or proclaiming a word that someone has not heard.
It may just be a smile for the one who for so many miles
has walked through the rain with teardrops of pain.

Or maybe it is for the holder of the napkin while eating a meal,
A note from God that shows his love and desire to heal.

For me it was this as I ate with friends an evening meal:

"God puts people in your life
When you need them.
For that we are thankful.
However, we always need
To also put God in our lives"

When we eat, when we play, when we pray
At all times if we listen God has something to say.

He finished his words with this reminder to me:

"I walk a fine line
Knowing the sign
When I go
That I know"

Reflection on Thoughts from a Green Paper Napkin Holder

We were having dinner with a group of friends and I had some thoughts about poems. I wrote them down on the paper napkin holder. This poem is the result of my wandering mind. I have been told since writing this that it is not a holder but a ring, that paper wrapping around the napkin wrapped silverware in restaurants.

The Dinner Table

At the end of the day, before the stars of night,
A family sits at a table, holding hands they pray,
Thanking the Lord for his bounty, the food they eat,
The hands they do hold, for all they receive.

Perhaps it is the first prayer a child does learn,
That all we need comes from his infinite love,
That the fruits of our labor are on the table,
And even more in our love for him and his children.

The family around the table shares their days,
Their joys, their sorrows, their hopes, their desires.
By starting their meal with a prayer
They have set the course for their lives.

At the table in God's sight
Seeds are sown that they always may
Share their blessing with those they meet,
To share God's grace that others may believe.

Praying, each in their turn,
They lift their thanks to the one above.
By this, as a family, they are able
To lift others from where they have been.

As a family together, each one prays
That they may live a life that God inspires,
As he encourages them to care
From the table to help others they leave.

It may be at the dinner table
That our faith may be shown
To our children as we pray,
Offering our thanksgiving,
And show them we are
Children of God
And together
We are part
Of God's family.

No Title, I know Not the Words

Out of thoughts, ideas, inspiration.
That crossed my mind as I lay wondering
What to write, if I was even right
About the words I no longer have.

I am out of thoughts, I have no idea
As my mind continues its wandering
From day break til the end of night.
Unrhyming words are all I have.

Then I realize that one word is out of place.
The thoughts and ideas are of me,
They are the visions that I see,
Thoughts and words without God's grace.

The word that does belong
Is the word for which I long.
It is inspiration, God's word through me
Of who I am with him, of what I can be.

Sometimes the poet thinks he is so smart.
With pen in hand and paper upon the desk
He sits to write words to inspire, but cannot start.
The ink does not flow, so words do not follow.

It is when he reflects on the times he did write,
Of the words that became verses as the ink did flow
That he remembers the times he did not fight
With unwritten ideas that the words did grow.

So he laid bare his soul, and knelt and prayed,
Thanking God for mending a life that was frayed,
For the gift of grace, for the gift of words,
The words given him when his mind was not blurred.

Lord, I ask today that you be my guide
In all I do, in all I desire be at my side,
But more I ask that I allow your spirit
To fill me with your word, that I hear it.

There Is Only One Rhyme That Will Last Beyond Time

From the beginning and until the end we
Have rebelled against our most Holy Father.
We have committed adultery with gods of wood
Thinking that for us they could provide good.

Prophets of Old Testament times have spoken
Of your anger at a people whose lives were broken,
Broken because their bond with you was torn
Long before so many were ever born.

John of the New Testament describes his revelation
Of the future of this world, of the end of nations.
We who are living in the grace of a new covenant
Have brought disgrace to the grace of his Providence.

What are we to do amid this turmoil
As the Heavens cry and our hearts boil?
How do we avoid God's anger, his wrath
As we continue down our destructive path?

Read his word, the scriptures both old and new.
Read his word, believe in his word and have life anew.
Though angry his love turned to blood,
His blood, that of his Son, that of his love.

If you believe in the God of the Bible,
You must believe his every word,
What he has done and what he will
Because of what we have done and will.

His ways are not our ways
And our ways are not his.
Be thankful that he loves us
More than we can ever love him.

He wanted us to be with him forever
So he sent his son to be the sacrifice,
To pay the price for the sins of many,
So that in his sight we are made right.

Read, believe, be baptized and spread his word.
Open your hearts to him so your soul may be saved,
That you may face eternity, not with foreboding,
But that you may face it forever with joy.

We know the story of the past,
Pray that we do not make it last,
Pray that the die has not been cast,
That at this time you accept his grace.

Since his Word spoke this world into existence,
Since that Word paid the ransom for our resistance,
Since before we were conceived in the womb
He knew us and desired that we avoid the tomb.

It is in our hands, the decision to be in his hands.
Get up from your life and with God stand.
Stand with faith in the resurrection of his Son
And our resurrection from what we have done.

God loves us.
He wants us with him.
He died once
That we might live.

Jesus rose so that we who believe
May also rise with him as we receive
All.

Reflection on There Is Only One Rhyme That Will Last Beyond Time

Every time I read the Bible I hope that God has a new poem to write. Sometimes it has been after reading only a few verses. This time it was after reading Jeremiah 14-16. I have been fascinated with end times prophecy for years. I am now more fascinated with the Old Testament prophets. I remember sitting with a small group in a 7 week session on Christ. The question was asked, does God ever get angry. Yes. I am glad that He loves and forgives. This poem is a continuation of the last poem in God's Rhyme, Broken Hearted. I wrote it on Dec. 30, 2014. When I finished the poem, God said that the book was done. I know now it was only the beginning.

Chapter Three, Taken From the Attic

Poems About You

I no longer have to write poems about you
you are my poetry
no more searching for rhymes
and worrying about the lines
in you I find
my words are to be spoken
the pen shant be broken
over any parchment
nor will the mind hinder the heart
as I have found
I no longer have to write
poems about you
you are all the poetry
that's been pent up inside of me
you are my rhyme
with time

For My Wife

you are my love
        everlasting and forever
what I need is all I desire
you have given me that
        and sealed it with gold

and I love you
        I love you because
        even when we are mad
        I so want to kiss you

and tell you I love you

I love you
brown eyes that smile
        when you are happy
smile when I am happy

the woman in you never
        steps on that little girl
who comes to visit once in awhile
        the angel who makes us both laugh

for laughing is love
our love is our happiness
        and happiness makes for laughing

Still untitled after all these years

funny how a woman takes your mind
and all of your time
        is spent on her
   and genius relinquishes itself
for a woman of that kind
    who you say is "mine"

and what if God himself had told you
    you already knew that time
        was yesterday
   and has given itself
into the hands of a woman
      you say is "mine"

there is nothing in a woman to find
        except your life
    and tomorrow is spent
          giving itself
to your care and love
     for a woman you say is "mine"

Homeward September

There is a woman who comes along
At times when I may be so wrong.
There is a woman I love so much
Who has love's sweet and tender touch.

A woman who cares about love and life,
Knowing that each, like the other is one,
Is what should be found in each man's life,
For in her, his battles are won.

A woman lends herself to all around,
A flower in bloom, a star at night.
With her is to be found
The end of the flight.

An open field lies ahead,
A universe to conquer is yours.
And through it all you may be led,
She'll never let you know it's anything but yours.

This woman so kind,
This woman of life,
This woman of mine,
This woman my wife.

Page 96, still untitled

To write a poem for you
is becoming
to me
    easier to do
as I learn to know
who you are
            wishing on a star
a locket
protecting you
from
    evil eyes
making me gaze
into
    your brown eyes

Whether sharing a chair
or
    ourselves
happiness
       fills the air
                  as I write
a poem for you
        again
still feeling warm
from the other night
            the fireplace
                your heart

Shall I sit near the
              warmth
of the fire
and never tire
       of
writing poems
       for you

Moments of Bridges

there is that moment
in some second of your life
when you know
she's the direction

the breeze was lightly
tumbling thoughts
around in my head
while aimlessly bouncing
was the beat of my heart
I knew so much
all of nothing
as the wind played gingerly
in my mind

and no sooner than
the wind had picked me up
it gave way to a still calm
of an aching loneliness
no more games with the playful wind
the moment in that second
changed its direction
as it hastened itself
on that same path to you

and now there
I think of the first
and that second
forever spent with you

Ships & Lakes & Me

You can sit on the beaches
Of the Great Lakes
And see tiny little ships
Sailing up and down.

By day in the distance
They are brown & black & white,
Sometimes indistinguishable
Little specs that
Are floating on the water.

By night, in the dark,
They are miniature lighted towns,
One here, another one there,
Moving, meeting & passing,
Sometimes in a line.

They are a beautiful sight,
Day or night,
Leaving a trace
Of smoke behind.

Sitting on the bank
Of the river St. Clair
The ships are life size,
So large and so real.

Reflection on Chapter 3 Poems

All of the poems in this chapter were written in the early 1970s. In the books God's Rhyme and God Still Rhymes I included poems that I had written earlier in my life.. Some were from unpublished manuscripts, some were just written, shared and then stored in the attic. Those in this chapter are that last from the attic I will publish. There are a lot more, most of which I like, but were written long before I met Jesus.

Chapter Four:
The End of The Days
for Writing a Book

This One Scares Me

Playing solitaire, telling God just one more game.
As usual my mind is abuzz with things of tomorrow.
I have an interview for God Still Rhymes,
I've done one before, I am with a friend.
Nothing to worry about with this wandering.

Then I ask a question, Lord what do you want me to do?
He answered, my dear son I have something for you.
My heart is still beating, my mind wondering why,
My heart telling me to stop the wondering, He is why.

The keys on the keyboard my fingers do not touch,
Not wanting to type anymore words and
Knowing that, knowing that I cannot say no.
No, it is finally my time to take a stand.

I had been thinking of a Bible study
Where there were those who had conversations with God.
And there I sat thinking I did not belong there
Because I had not, was there something in me odd?

But here I am today
Writing of God's ways
That when I pray
I hear his voice
And he hears mine.

His voice giving me the letters.
Forming the words,
Continually forming my soul
That in his way he will make me better.

I have conversations with him,
We occasionally sing a hymn.
He's everywhere
If I am aware.

Lord take away my anxiety,
Let me not worry about the rhymes,
Open the door to this cavern in which I live
So I am open to all that you have to give.

The Prophets of Yesterday, Are They Heard Today?

*Jeremiah 18:10, They said, "Come let's make plans
against Jeremiah; for the teaching of the law by the priest
will not cease, no will counsel from the wise,
no the word from the prophets. So come, let's attack him
with our tongues and pay no attention to anything he says."*

Thousands of years ago the people of God did rebel,
Forgetting their fears, from his righteous protection they fell,
There were warnings of God's anger in their rebellion
Yet the storming clouds of his anger were ignored.

Today as we read God's word we learn
How his people suffered for what they did earn;
Separation from the love God had for those
He loved, the very ones who for generations he chose.

Those very same prophets also foretold
Of a time with a promise to come,
A promise from God ever so bold,
That a there would be salvation through a son.

Here we are today living with that prophecy,
The Lamb of God born and living among us,
Showing the way that so many would see,
See you, Lord, in the God man Jesus.

And while on this earth Jesus told of our future,
What lies ahead for a world that refuses
To heed his call, to not see the fall
Caused by our rebellion, our rejection.

We read books explaining the end of days.
Do we who are saved continue to pray?
Do we ever tell others of our evil ways
And what we know his word does say?

We are sometimes uncomfortable talking our faith.
Not always comfortable as we come face to face
With another who has yet to hear of God's grace.
Do we sometimes wither from our faith?

I wonder if given the choice what would I chose;
To speak of salvation and pray for another's soul
And leave my faith there with nowhere to go.
Or would I chose to walk toward the goal?

Am I willing to be the one the world does mock
Because it is only in themselves they take stock,
To continue the story to the very end,
Knowing that my words God will defend?

If I have the love of God dwelling in me,
If I believe he has sent the Holy Spirit
To guide and direct me, to live for you,
Then follow his will I must do.

I will tell of the end of days,
The result of our evil ways,
I will tell of his righteous wrath
As the world follows an evil path.

I will tell of his glorious gift of grace,
A grace with which the world cannot rhyme
As we continue to shutter the doors
To the truth, the way and the light.

Jesus commanded us to spread the gospel.
To honor him we must do it completely.
God will comfort us as we are uncomfortable.
Through his Spirit the full story we can tell.

Is This The Human Condition
(This is not a question)

Where is God when we need him?
Why has this happened again,
Over and over again?
We were told you were a good God,
A loving God who cares for his people.
Where are you in our times of need!

Before our time of need
We should take time to read
Of the history of his chosen ones,
His beloved daughters and sons.

In their times of greed
They did not see the need
To honor his glory and heed
His word, words that feed.

It is there for us today.
Did we not know so we cannot say?
Did we not know as we walked away
That you despised our way?

Did we not hear that Jesus came,
Not just for the Jew, but also the Gentile?
He came so that with God we could reconcile
So as Jew and Gentile we are all the same.

If we love God and his Son,
No matter what we have done,
His love for us is never ending.
Our lives forever he will be mending,

If we love him we must follow
With words and prayers not hollow,
We must be true to him who loves us,
Loves us so much he sacrificed Jesus.

There is a reason us rhymes with Jesus.

But we never learned the lesson,
Maybe because we never read
Of God's anger over the adultery
Of his chosen ones with idols
And false gods, the gods of others
That do no good, but only harm.
Gods of wood and gold, some were so bold
To worship nothing instead of everything,
All that their God had for them.

So where is God today as children are slaughtered,
As lives are abandoned and hope forgotten?
He is everywhere, where are we?

Reflection on Is This the Human Condition

I think that I mentioned before that I had no idea what direction the book I am writing here would lead me. Although I talk of reading God's word and receiving the words of the poems from God, I am probably the last person, if I were on the outside looking in, that I would think could have that relationship. It has grown since I started writing this book. But the poems continue to surprise and amaze me. I was reading. Hosea before writing and I just stopped and wondered at the times God's chosen people walked away from Him and then when trouble came, well you know what we all do at those times. Today we are in the same place. I had no idea what I would write other than the title.

As Only You Can

I look at the clouds and I wonder aloud
What lies beyond the skies?
What ever can be though looking I cannot see.
I look at the wonder of it all and I hear your call.

Beyond the skies is Heaven above,
Where there are no whys, just your love.
But first we share in this world of ours
For what we care in each day's hours.

The mountains, the valleys,
The meadows, the deserts,
And the vast deep waters,
They all exist inside of us.

You spoke the earth into existence,
You breathed your breath into man,
Your power knew no resistance.
It was only and is only you who can.

May we live in your glory,
Be a part of your story.
May we every day strive
To have you in our lives.

May we see the splendor,
Of all you do, of who we are
As we shine brighter than the stars
When we let you, Lord, be who you are.

Corners

I lay curled up in the corner
. . . . . . of a round room.
Every few days I move
to another corner
in the round room.
Without any windows.
There would be such gloom
In the corners of a round room.

Sure, not everything I have said
. . . . rhymes,
But in a round room
It is hard to get your thoughts straight.
Letters and vowels and syllables
Never stop as they circle time
faster than the hours pass.

A day of this kind
Is sometimes in my mind,
The days that I find
Where nothing rhymes.

Why, I don't have to ask.
I have forgotten the task
I must perform to find the door,
To find that there is more
Than the corners of a round room,
To overcome my sense of gloom.

As I circle in doubt
I know the way out.
But I must submit

So he can commit
To open the door
So I may get off the floor.

I must knock on the wall
So that I will hear his call.
And he will hear as I knock
And make the door that he opens.
I must remember there is no lock
To his love behind the door he opens

Reflection on Corners

This is me all too often.

For Those He Loves

There are words of our feelings
And words for our healing.
There are arms that embrace
As life's threads we lace.

For him his life was more than touched,
It was ravaged by cancer,
An ugly uncaring disease
For those it reaches out and touches.

But somehow through all of the pain,
When all around the skies just rain,
Though not knowing the future
There always was hope in love.

It was in a book about a young boy
Who was born inside out.
The story told of his growing from toys
Of childhood to the toys of his children.

There was love in a poem on a brown paper bag.
There was love in the air that made him aware
That with this girl he could not let time drag.
The love she gave him was all he wanted to share.

There were children, not one but five,
So every day he knew that he was alive.
Family, oh the love they would give
Each and every day he did live.

The story continued through the love of sadness,
When life gave those who were there at his birth,
When it was their lives that were turned inside out,
When happiness and hope appeared much less.

First one, then the other,
Married for so many years
They suffered together
As others watched through tears.

Surgery the first invasion for both.
Then the invasion to their system
Of perhaps lifesaving drugs.
Then the burning sensation
Of man's treatment of radiation.
All ending, all ending at the end.

The amazing part of the story was
The continuation of love that surrounded
Those sick and those tired watching the sickness.
The rhymes were there though written
With different words, in different lines.

The chapter on cancer ended, the story went on.
The author of life had healed the broken hearts
With words of hope and his blessings of love.
That inside out boy was made right
By the love of God and his sight
Was restored so that he might
Continue his life in God's love.

The story is one of love.
Love for others, love for God
And the love God had for them all
As he continued to heed God's call.

God's rhyme is everywhere,
In the good, the bad of all we see and do.
His rhymes are always there
If we are open, not just to what it is he can do,
But believing he will always care.

Draw Me Closer

Dear Lord, draw me closer to you
In all I desire in all I do.
Lord, open my heart to your Holy Spirit,
Your spirit that dwells within me.
Lord, I do not want to knock on the door
So that you may open it for me,
I want the door to always be open.
I never want it to close.
Those moments when we share
My prayers and your answers
Are special moments I pray
Will never end, but continue
Throughout my day.
With the door open
I allow you to lead me from temptation,
I allow myself to be in your presence,
One with you, Abba, Father.
Abba, that relationship
I pray will never end.
Thank you, Father
For leading me to
The way,
The truth
And the life
With you
Through your Son, Jesus.
Amen.

Meet Me

Lord, meet me, set me free.
You know where I've been, you know of my sin.
And although you know, you continue to show
That I am your child with a love so mild.

Lord, you met me when I could not see
Beyond my sight, what I thought was right.
You met me in the dirt of my earthly hurt.
My life you did raise so that you I could praise.

Finally found, hearing your sound,
The whisper of your spirit, loud enough that I did hear it.
You met me in uncharted seas with the waves washing over me
And calmed the storms in a life forlorn.

My Morning Prayer:

Meet me, Lord, every day
As I lift my head from my bed.
Help me to pray that each new day
I hear you before rising to my feet.

You, Lord, are my anchor,
You are my healer,
You are my redeemer,
My hope,
My joy.
You, Lord,
Are my everything.

Without you, Lord, I am nothing.
With you I can be everything
You want me to be,
Everything that you have for me.

My Evening Prayer:

May my life be as unleavened bread,
Without the yeast as the world serves it,
So when we meet I can hear the words said,
Well done, my good and faithful servant.

The Gentleness of Faith

Our faith is a reflection
That upon recollection
By those whose lives we passed.
Will see a love that lasts.

Our faith is not quarrelsome,
We speak in gentle tones
To those who do not know the Son
So they see the love he has shown.

His spirit may raise our voice,
Though never in anger, but in joyful song
Of a love that will make eyes moist
As the lost find that for which they do long.

Love is gentle in its forgiving
As shown by how we were living,
That as Christ redeemed us at the cross
So now we may live without the loss,

The loss of,
The love of his promise,
The gift of his grace,
That with Christ we will rise
When his call will end our race.

For God so loved us he gave his only Son
So we could join him and be the ones
To share,
To care,
To be there,
Anywhere

He calls,
Standing tall
So others hear
There is no fear
In God's embrace
As the world we face.

Without love for others,
For our sisters and brothers,
Our faith is but mist in the air.
So how to the lost do we share?

Pray that our faith leaves no question
Of who God is and who we are in him.
May the gentle love of God
Be the gentleness of our faith.

Reflection on The Gentleness of Faith

I was led, or more likely I meandered, through four books before getting the inspiration for this poem. It came from 2 Timothy 2:24.

And the Lords servant must not be quarrelsome
But must be kind to everyone, able to teach, not resentful.

Talk Around the Table

As he was walking toward the table
The others were already talking
As the smell of food was in the air
And the mood at the table was good.

And of course he thought
Why doesn't good rhyme with food
But mood does with one
But not the other?
It was hard to be understood.

But he found as he listened to the sound
Of their voices talking as he was walking
There are rhymes that at times,
Rhymes heard without the sound of a voice.

One comment turned the talk to God.
Admittedly for lunch talk this was odd.
There were believers and there were not,
But calm prevailed and the talk did not get hot.

Oh sure sometimes it was out of sync
As someone took time to think
Of what to say next and not perplex
Those around the table, if one was able.

What started as a freewheeling talk fest
Where one never was made to feel like a guest
The talk turned to a serious conversation,
A discussion of God and man's salvation.

Through it all it was a comfortable time
Where occasionally the yours and mine
Differed, but never led to a division
That can be caused by one or the other's decision.

We listened with open ears
And some spoke of their fears
While some spoke in quiet tones
That Jesus' love is what atones.

There was this and that among the chit chat
And a good share of that was of God's care
From our beginning and beyond our end,
All of this around the table of friends.

And as we left there was one who beamed
Because of questions that were answered.
The conversation planted the seed it seemed
Because he knew one would follow to water.

Reflection on Talk Around the Table
This happened at work one day.

Days of Discouragement

He woke up to a buzzing alarm,
Though startled, it did him no harm.
Sitting up he stretched his arms
As like bees thoughts came in swarms.

This day wasn't yesterday
So he did kneel and pray
That he would find God's way
And there he would stay.

Preparing himself for the day ahead
Hoping that . . .

Suddenly,
The day came crashing down instead.
The rhyme was gone,
Thoughts became thoughtless,
Words had no sounds.

Then walking through an open door
As he wished, not hoped, for something more,
He saw someone he knew,
Who yesterday he had talked to.

It wasn't that the person was there
That brought him to reality.
It was the question that was asked
That made him stop and stare.

The question was a reflection
Of that person's recollection
Of yesterday's sharing of God's word
And his hoping it had been heard.

It had been heard and the questions spilled out.
And as he answered one after another one
He could feel his spirt rising up, wanting to shout.
He knew before the end what God had done.

It wasn't that God had put someone on the path,
The path he was taking today.
No, God had placed someone in his way,
Someone needing to know how to follow God's path.

It wasn't a believer,
Though it was someone
In fear of the deceiver,
With questions about God's Son.

And in that moment of time
He found in his voice the sound
Of God's Holy Spirit filling the lines
In his answers with God's rhymes.

God works in many ways.
And who are we to say
What or who God can use
So that him we do not lose?

God heals those who are broken,
Sometimes with the words spoken
By those who do not know him
But need you to show them.

With God discouragement
Becomes encouragement.

Reflection on Days of Discouragement

This was the day at work after Talk Around the Table.

A Writer's Confession

A Catholic priest explained confession in this way:
First we admit to ourselves that we have sinned,
Then we confess to God that we have sinned,
Finally the confessional is a public confession that we have sinned.

That was over forty years ago and as some may know
Sometimes memories become hazy, though not because we are lazy.
If I remember this wrong I confess to all now
That I am mistaken in remembering the why and how.

Raised as an Episcopalian,
A converted Catholic,
A husband and father of five,
Then decades later led to leave,
To venture out on my own
To find the place God wanted me to be.

This may be longer
As my desire becomes stronger
To unload my soul
To help plug the hole
That has haunted,
That has daunted
Me for years
Filled with fears
And too many tears.

Okay, so much for rhyming,
I'm losing my timing.
The length of the lines
Don't matter sometimes.

What ever makes someone think
That they have something to share,
Think that anyone will really care?
Your words on the page may be overlooked
In the blink of an eye, in the sight
Of other pages by someone else,
Pages that for them may be more right.

There are others who as experts write
Of what is true with the force of might,
A strength that comes through to the reader
That the author in his field is a leader.

There are those who study and research.
For the answers we seek they do search.
These writers even I will seek out
To relieve my fears and doubt.

But I confess who I am, one who has wandered
From here to there, many times without care,
Who am I, what have I to share
In living this life I have squandered?

I write of me, of the things I see.
The emotions I feel
Of a life that is real,
I write of life of words that is me.

Alone if I wrote
With nothing to quote,
As I write of my pain
It would all be in vain.

One day a long time ago I was introduced to God.
One day a long time ago lasted for so many years.
With introductions made, God began to lead the way
And blind as I was I followed without seeing.

Then came years where the lines
In Amazing Grace were a reflection of me.
Admitting my sin, God saved a wretch like me.
Then followed days in and out of his rhymes.

With further years I realized the writing
Was a gift from God as he was righting
My life, my heart, my love for him.
He loved and guided me even through my sin.

I have a terrible memory, find it hard to memorize.
Yes, I know I should pray to be able to recite
The words he has given us to overcome life's lies,
To overcome my fear of not getting it right.

But God has given me a gift, a gift he chose,
That I should tell a story of my life
Through the wretched times of strife
And the life I have with him as from death Jesus rose.

I have expressed that the words you read are not mine,
But the words that God tells me to write with my own hand.
I am convinced that even as I wrote as I sinned
The words were from God, and not this mortal man.

I hope that I never take pride in this
Because it is only by the guidance of his
Spirit that I can write my name at the end
Of words given, with a heart he does mend.

I confess to you dear reader
That if anyone is imperfect it is me.
But now I accept that God did see
The writer he wanted others to read.

Through two books and a couple of manuscripts unpublished I have been blessed in knowiing the love of God more than I ever thought possible. To write I must read, just as you, dear reader do to know what God has done for you, to know of your salvation, to know what it is he wants you to do.

So in my doubt I have found out
Why I write words I have heard
And why the rhymes are used so many times.
It is the Holy Spirit who helps me hear it.

An Eternal Heart

Therefore we do no lose heart.
Though outwardly we are wasting away,
yet inwardly we are being renewed day by day.
2 Corinthians 4:16

As our years pass our outer body shows age.
In the book we write of life every year turns a page,
But with God every day our soul he renews.
The outside and inside present different views.

For our light and momentary troubles are
achieving for us and eternal glory
that far outweighs them all. 2 Corinthians 4:17

In the earthly life we live we will face
Trials and troubles that will test our faith.
It is in each trial and trouble that we find
An answer from God that is beyond our mind
To understand because his ways are not ours.
He loves us all for all time through all the hours.

The strength of our faith will grow
As his seeds God does sow,
Seeds of love for him in those who are meek
So that at all times, in all things it is him that we seek.

So we fix eyes not on what is seen,
but on what is unseen,
since what is seen is temporary,
but what is unseen is eternal.
2 Corinthians 4:18

It is only with God that we can look at the unseen
With the hope and promise that goes beyond our being.
We have the promise through Jesus, God's Son,
That after our death, for eternity with him we will be one.

We live in a temporary state in these jars of clay
Knowing that we will be with God at the end of our days.
Through eternity and beyond we will be forever
With our Heavenly Father, we will live forever

Inspired By Babies

There are long times and short lines,
Times of rhymes and times without,
But throughout time we have much to learn
As when they cry, when they laugh our heads turn.

I have seen the birth of five,
Felt their first breath,
I heard their first cry,
Never did I ask why
Until now.

This I know,
They are a miracle.
We may be at the end,
But they continue the circle
Of birth,
Rebirth,
Death and
Resurrection.

Babies are one of God's rhymes,
Rhymes written in free verse,
No two the same, but still they are one,
A gift from God forever in time.

We go out of our way to talk to them,
To hold and comfort them with a smile.
We will do this forever, not just awhile.
And as they are broken we will help them mend.

A gift from God, these little ones,
All his children, daughters and sons.
In their birth we find our worth
In our Father's love as we live on this earth.

Each newborn baby is special in God's sight.
Then we are reborn and made righteous in his sight
If we accept the sacrifice made by his Son
For our life of sin and the wrong we have done.

But, do we ever look at our neighbor
Or the stranger we see on the street?
Do we ever think to stop our feet
Just to ask, "do you know your savior?"

If we can look at a newborn with awe and wonder,
Why do we see others and only see thunder?
Will lightning strike if we talk to a child
Who with added years seems less mild?

When does God's awe and wonder end?
He breathed life into the first man, Adam,
Of whom we all are offspring.
We are all created by the Breath of Life.

That person on the street with clothes tattered and torn
May be that newborn whose life is now worn,
Tattered and worn out by a world of doubt.
Do we not see the awe and wonder inside the clothes?

God loves us and wants us to be with him.
A God of care and wonder created us all,
From that newborn we all grow in our sin.

Like a newborn that life tattered and torn
Cries in the night, needs a loving embrace,
We are called to comfort God's lost children,
To give them our hand, to help them stand tall
So with ears opened they hear God's call

Reflection on Inspired by Babies

I finished typing this to a waking baby's cry. I typed as I wrote.

The Veil Torn, the Presence of God

A Time Before
*An when Jesus had cried out again
in a loud voice, he gave up his spirit.
At that moment the curtain in the temple
was torn in two from top to bottom.
Matthew 27: 50,51*

The veil in the Temple of the Old Testament
Concealed the Holy of Holies, the place
where the Ark of the Covenant
and God's presence rested.

One time each year the priest entered
To offer atonement for the sins of God's people.

Then Today
*The veil is taken away. But whenever
Anyone turns to the Lord, the veil is taken away.
2 Corinthians 3:16*

The veil was torn, God's presence now shown
To those who believe in his atonement for our sin.
It is now through Jesus that we see the face of God,
That we can live in his presence, that his face is known.
Jesus is the high priest that sits at God's right hand
Making intercession for us as our prayers we present.
It is through his atonement for our sin that we now stand
Knowing that through his Son, we are always in God's presence.

If we accept God's gift,
The grace of his love,
The death of his Son

In a way that by us
Could never be done,
We will not see the veil,
We will see only his love.

We now come to God through Jesus
Who lived facing the temptations
We live with each and every day.
He understands our weaknesses.

Now and Forever
Therefore, since we have a great high priest
who has ascended into heaven, Jesus, the Son
of God, let us hold firmly to the faith we profess.
For we do not have a high priest who is unable
to empathize with our weaknesses, but we have
one who has been tempted in every way,
just as we are — yet he did not sin.
Let us then approach God's throne of grace
with confidence, so that we may receive mercy
and find grace to help us in our time of need.
Hebrews 4:14-16

It is through Jesus that we are now able to be in God's presence.

Thoughts from Reading Peter

I just finished reading 1 Peter
And I am continually reminded
That the Bible is as much about today
As it is about yesterday,
And it is much about tomorrow
As it is about all of our todays
As it is about all of the yesterdays.

As I read I wondered about tomorrow
And what may lead to our sorrow,
But then I remembered that tomorrow
Will worry about itself.
We are told not to worry
So why do we have to hurry
To get through today?
Maybe I need to pray.

No matter where I have read
God's word it has kept me fed.
I just have to remember
That as a family member
I live with God, through his grace.

I may fail today in so many ways,
But with God, tomorrow is a new day.

Chef Shell's

As you open the door you hear the bell ringing,
Voices are talking sounding like a quiet choir singing.
Come early for a breakfast donut, maybe jelly,
Or maybe you will have two to fill your belly.

Sorry, a poet tries to rhyme when possible,
Although that sometimes it is impossible.

Not a morning person, try lunch.
Maybe you're a mid-morning riser,
Then for you it will probably be brunch,
Or early dinner for the later survivor.

Whether you are wide eyed and bushy tailed
Or sleepy eyed and your boat has not yet sailed,
You are welcomed by a welcoming staff
Who are always ready at your jokes to laugh.

An atmosphere of comfort,
With service served with smiles,
Smiles that are real
Because they know the meal
They serve is all you need
To satisfy the hunger you feed.

And sometimes sitting in the corner
Is a quiet old man with books to sell.
You see him just past the ringing bell.
Some may think he is a foreigner.

But from times before he knows
That as the hungry hungrily ate
The eaters would glance at a table with books,
They glance but try to keep from staring looks.
But there are times their interest grows
And books he sells, maybe seven or eight,

But usually more.

Chef Shell's, a place built on love,
Love for what they do,
Love for me, love for you.
Enjoy and come back often
So maybe you can see
The man in the corner use his pen.

No, not everything has to rhyme to be good.
(Just like food.)

Reflection on Chef Shell's

I wrote this after they hosted my fourth book signing. They hosted my first ever book signing for God's Rhyme. They have been a blessing.

The Daily Eclipse

Yesterday part of the world stood still
As the sun, the moon and the earth
Moved in a way they seldom will.

Many took time out of their day
To observe the moon block out the sun,
To block the magnificence of its rays.

Slowly moving the three spheres,
Celestial bodies in the sky,
The world asked how, but not why.

And we all looked in amazement
At an occasional occurrence
Because it is so very rarely sent.

As we stare at the sun blocked sky
Do we ever wonder about
Not just the how, but the why?

Are we ever aware of more than the sun?
Are we aware of the daily eclipse of our lives
As the world blocks the light of God's Son?

The Light of the world is darkened
As we continue to lose our sight
In a world that knows not wrong or right.

May every day we live be with the light
Of God in our lives so we are never blinded
By the darkness.

Reflection on The Daily Eclipse

This was written on August 22, 2017 after the full solar eclipse. I couldn't help but think that the world we live in too often is an eclipse of our view of God and His goodness.

Do Not Let Me Sit

I sit with pen in hand because it is too hard to stand.
I sit in the chair looking up in the air.
I think that I know, but is it really so?
And I realize that for thoughts to materialize
Praying to you is what I must do.

Lord, I love you, I really do.
I do not wish, but hope instead
That I can pray and clear my head
So that today all I desire is you.

I am what I am, I do not like to hear,
For that to be true, I must abandon you.
I am what I am, that I greatly fear,
If that is so, then I have not been made anew.

My prayer, Lord, is that I let you be
Who you are, so that what you see in me
Is more that I am alone, but all that I am with you.
It is only by your grace that with me you are not through.

And as I place my trust in you I see each line is longer
As my faith, my love, my hope in you, Lord, gets stronger.
Lord, with you I know there is no danger
That one day we may become strangers.

Lord,
Help me to pray every day,
To read your word and know what I have heard.
Help me to spread your good news to more than a few,
To more than those sitting in the pew not knowing what to do.
Lead me to those, the ones you chose
To hear of you and all that you have done.

May every day be the beginning
Of showing others that winning
In life need not be full of stress,
Not when you, Lord, are here to bless.

Thank you, Lord, that these words
That rhyme have a reason.
That the thoughts that are written
Will always be in season.

For it is with you, Father, that our lives are full,
That when we care, it is you that we share.

Whose Words

And this is my prayer; that your love may abound
more and more in knowledge and depth of insight,
so that you may be able to discern what is best
and may be pure and blameless for the day of Christ,
filled with the fruit of righteousness that comes
Jesus Christ – to the glory and praise of God.
Phil 1:9,10

Whose words do we seek
As we hear others speak?
Are they the words of truth
That in us will bear fruit?

As believers do we know God's word
Or do we only know what we have heard?
Do we ever make the time to know
What God's word says so we may grow?

Do we have the desire to understand
Where it is God wants us to stand?
Do we search his word, do we make the time to study
So that when someone speaks we are not just putty?

Do we know when the words are from God and not from man?

To understand your word we must have a yearning
To listen to others and not overlook our own learning.
Through prayer and reflection in our time alone
With you, Father, we will mature in our love for the cornerstone.
The cornerstone of your church, of our faith, your Son Jesus,
Is fully known as we seek in your word how you see us.
We must read so we know the truth when we hear it
And know what is not from you so we may not be near it.

You, Lord, love us every day
So every day we must pray
That as we read we know what you say
About the truth of your grace and your way.

Thank you, Lord, for what you do,
Help us to be more than just a few,
Help us to know and spread your word
So others cannot say they never heard.

I Have Nothing

I have nothing to add to the word of God.
I have nothing to add to his love for me.
I have nothing to offer to make me worthy.
I have nothing to add to God's rhymes.

That is true, but . . .
I can believe in His word.
I can accept his love for me.
I can accept that through Jesus I am worthy.
I can become one of God's rhymes.

I can offer my life to God.
I can spread the Good News of salvation.
I can be a reflection of his love.
I can share the end of the Christmas story.

I have nothing on my own to give to God,
But with God I have everything to give.
I have every reason to live for him.
I have hope for life eternal with him.

I have nothing until I have God in my life,
Until I accept the atoning sacrifice
That showed his love for me.
I can accept Jesus, my savior,
My redeemer, my hope, my everything.

Thoughts on the Way to Church

The lost sheep,
Are we led,
Led to the way
Or led astray,
Are we fed
By the Bread of Life
Or captive to strife

There are random thoughts that cross my mind
That make me seek the words to find
That will feed me and lead me
To the right words to write

No questions,
No exclamations
Period?

Just the question,
As lost sheep are we led,
As lost sheep are we fed
To the truth, by the truth
Of who God is,
What Jesus has done
And the mission
Of the Holy Spirit?

Do we ever question God's love?
Do we ever shout an exclamation?
Or do we just end with a period?

God's love for us is never in question,
We should shout to the world in exclamation
That with God our lives will not end with a period.

The Book on the Shelf

I asked the Lord, what do I write
He replied, write of yourself
Take the book of your life off the shelf
Open you heart and turn on the light

So, here I am, where have I misplaced that book
The many nooks and crannies where I have looked
Were empty, as if they had been visited by a crook
When did I last use it, that memory someone took

I prayed, Lord, show me what I have missed
At which he led me through a fine and foggy mist
To the place on a shelf
Where I found myself.

Sometimes I close the cover to my life
And then I find that every day is a fight
As I fail to follow the light he has shining on me
A light that does reflect from him so that I can see

I have these days when I lose my way
When the world around me tears at my heart
When the world around me leads me astray
When I awake sleepy eyed at the day's new start

Maybe it was a word, a thought, a slight I did perceive
Something I was unprepared that day to receive
Maybe it was just me
Maybe I just didn't see

The book on the shelf is where I was found
The book where the story of my life is bound
Where God placed me to keep me safe
As the world around me runs its race

Sometimes I get off track in the race I run
When I confuse God's blessings with earthly fun
When I get caught in life's struggles before the day is done
When I distract myself from the life I have with God's Son

My story is one of God's love for me
A story of his infinite grace in my life
His forgiving of my many wanderings
A story of my faith in God and his in me

Reflection on The Book on the Shelf
There is no punctuation when the day is a run on sentence
A sentence without bars, but one that can easily become a prison.

Another Day

I was sound asleep
Not making a peep,
Not snoring out loud,
My head in a cloud.

Then there was a shout.
What was that all about?
Now awake I got out of bed
And, what else, hit my head.

Looking up I found
The source of that sound,
The cause of all my harm,
A clock with a buzzing alarm.

Oh my,
I asked why
Was today
Starting this way.

Looking up as I lay on the floor
I see a figure standing at the door.
What else, was there anything more?
My goodness it was only four!

Good afternoon, my wife said to me.
I guess you forgot your glasses and couldn't see
That A M and P M are as different as day and night.
You have not only lost your mind, but also your sight.

The sight of my mind,
If that I could find,
I could remember time
And find that watch of mine.

Somehow with bare feet and my soul now bare
I made it to the kitchen where I became aware
That all I needed was a little Dr. Pepper
And a whole lot of Jesus

Reflection on Another Day

I had been bewildered for few days by the Facebook page, another book and things. I thought I needed a rest from posting every day. And I must admit to becoming discouraged as the number of views dropped. I think I know why. I listened to my wife a few nights before and then found that God told her to talk to me. I had been reading from the beginning of Genesis, then ended up taking an unplanned nap. My cell phone woke me up and then the first two stanzas of this poem came to me. It was fun to write and hope you found it fun to read. That night I found that all I need is a rhyme and a whole lot of Jesus.

Yesterday Today and Tomorrowday

As I write this it is today.
I wrote the one for yesterday
Sometime earlier today.
You will read this tomorrowday.

Yeah, it sounds nonsensical.
Maybe it's like something from
A long lost, thankfully, musical
Whose tunes you cannot hum.

For some that is the total sum
Of a week of days ever so weak;
There was yesterday's yesterday
And then tomorrowday's tomorrowday.

But we must remember the times
When writing of the week's rhymes
That spellcheck continues to tell us we that we are wronger
With those red squiggly lines under words that are stronger.
(Writers comment: Man versus machine, God always wins.)

One day tomorrowday will be yesterday.
We cannot worry about whatever day
We find ourselves living in,
Whether we lose or we win.

As we face each day we must pray,
Pray aloud that God removes the cloud
Of doubt so we may shout
For the world to hear that we have no fear.

Yes, we will have our coffee,
We will have the lives we live,
But these things become small
When we answer God's call.

Yesterday I wrote, and today I write
As I will tomorrowday write,
"All I need today is a little Dr. Pepper
And a whole lot of Jesus"

Pray that we may
Stay with him always,
That what we say
May reflect the way
He has saved us,
God's Son, Jesus.

Meaningless Words

First came the revulsion,
Followed by the revolution
That was followed by the revolt
That struck like a lightning bolt.

These are but words written on a page,
Knowing that I am certainly no sage.
Who could ever imagine the rage
That is not a performance on a stage?

Just words, what do they mean?
Is it more or less than they seem?
Or maybe it is just a movie scene
Or a restless night time dream.

Did anyone read as if they cared
As meaningless words were shared?
Is there something not written,
Words that need to be spoken?

They live with revolution
As so many live to revolt
Against God's judgement,
Expecting a deferment.

The lightning bolt will appear in the skies
As those who have lived to deny
Will suddenly have a need to rely
On their creator to hear their cries.

We who have believed will be relieved
Because we received and were not deceived.
There is good and evil, the fruit of the tree.
But the Lord fed our hunger and set us free.

As the world rebelled
Nations were felled,
After which His word prevailed
Until again false words were regaled.

We who believe in Jesus, God's Son,
At the end our lives will not have to run
From the lives we lived and what we have done,
We will be saved, our redemption has been won.

As others fight against what is right,
They are blind to the light, blind without sight,
They may live, but what they give
Is a meaningless word, because they have not heard.

Too busy in their confusion
Of living for the revolution
They do not hear
That God is near.

As we approach the end
We do not need life insurance,
We need life assurance,
The salvation that God sends!

Reflection on Meaningless Words

This poem started after an afternoon of going over words that rhyme in my head. I had written a poem in the morning and found that joy and satisfaction of writing again. The first three stanzas came to me as I was watching TV. I had to get paper and a pencil so I would not forget the words. I wrote of this problem in a book years ago, the title of which explains everything, I Can't Remember the Things I Forgot. It was short with a lot of blank pages. Ok, back to the poem. After making a grilled cheese sandwich I asked for guidance and the words to make sense of my thoughts. This is it, a collaboration between God and me. But somehow I am sure He was there at the beginning and through the whole poem.

What Have I Done for You?

There are those days when the sky is blue.
And then there comes that one day
When the sky is filled with clouds of gray.
On that day what have I done for you?

It is easy to talk as through life we walk,
To share the smiles as we walk the miles,
As we walk that mile that once in awhile
Is filled with pain as the gray clouds rain.

It is that mile that I must be aware
That even though I know you are there
That you need more from me.
You need me to help you see.

I have walked that mile alone
When my heart has turned to stone.
I have stumbled along that road
Struggling with my life's heavy load.

It is at these times of being in need
I do not want what I know I need.
It is then that I need someone
To remind me of God's Son.

So as we walk under skies of gray,
It is then that I need to pray,
Pray, not alone, but with you
That you may see the sky of blue.

I need to let you know
That there is a rainbow
Above the day's gray cloud
That is like a darkened shroud.

I will take your hand and pray
That we will not be led astray,
That as we walk we will talk
And let God's reign fall on us.

Reflection on What Have I Done for You

I know that I need to pray for other's needs, but there are times that I need to pray with them.

Drinking After Ten

It is after ten and the sky is dark
I sit and think that I should write
I should pray that this is not a lark
Knowing of they demon I must fight

My father was an alcoholic
Of this I have written before
There is no rhyme for that word
So I will not even try to find one

He would sit at the dining room table
Where he could watch the TV
With a glass in front of him for all to see
I now wonder if he was ever able

Able to know or even care
That he life he did share
With those who loved him
Knew the demon of his sin

As he drove to work there was a bottle under the seat
Always opened and ready, protected by his feet
And I remember the time he came home late
Because after driving off the road, coffee saved his fate

Back in the day as people like to say
Driving drunk was less offensive
If nothing was hurt except your ride home
But not your pride when couldn't have known
There were a wife and sons always waiting
Wishing they weren't always hating
The uncertainty of the unknown
The brokenness of seeds once sown

Did it kill him, yes it did
The how is something that hid
Hid for so many years
That it brought more than tears

Worse than all of our fears
Alcoholism spread like a cancer
That in the end took his life
A blessing that took from him his strife

So I sit here tonight
And I wonder what might
Happen to me
If . . .

Who could foresee
What would ever be
Only God could ever have known
The seeds that were then sown

Labor Days

As followers of Christ we are his day laborers,
Laboring every day and through the night.
In first Corinthians we are told to
Always give ourselves to the Lord's work
Because we know that our labor
In the Lord is never in vain.

The wages of our sin were ransomed
By a death on the cross so our loss
Would not be forever, that never
Would we be forsaken, forever.

The one who plants and the one who waters
have one purpose, and they will each be
rewarded according to their own labor.
for we are co-workers in God's service;
you are God's field, God's building. 1Cor, 3:8,9

We work, but our toil is not with the soil.
The seeds one plants are the seeds of God's love.
The one who waters does so with the living water
Of a death, a resurrection, of forgiveness and love.

For we are God's handiwork,
created in Christ Jesus to do good works,
which God prepared in advance for us to do."
Eph, 2:10

By God's grace we have been saved by faith
To perform the good works he has prepared for us.
We receive our reward through God's Son, Jesus.
And as we have received we must help others believe.

We labor in love,
The love of God,
Our love for our neighbor,
The love for our Savior
So that others will see
What with God they can be.

Yes, at times a grueling task,
But God did not just ask,
No it is a command we must follow
Unless we think any of his words are hollow.

He prepared the works to be done
Knowing we have strength through his Son.
We must labor for God in this life we live.
Just consider the sacrifice for us he did give.

Labor Day, a holiday for man to celebrate the worker's labor.
Let us make every day a holy day and celebrate,
Let us celebrate and not worry or contemplate,
But let us pray for all things as for God we do labor.

Reflection on Labor Days

Yes, I did labor on this poem. And I was given a revelation. I got out my Pocket Rhyming Dictionary so I could have more variety in my rhymes. There is no section for the letter L and a few others. I am satisfied with the rhymes God has.

The Next Step of Promises

A lone figure was walking along a trail,
In the heat of the shining sun he looked frail
To those he passed on his way somewhere.
Where, he would know when he got there.

Walking from the desert he looked to the sky,
But unlike those he had passed he knew why.
He looked not with questions, no he understood,
That his next step would lead to all that is good.

Before him was a mountain to ascend.
He knew that to reach the summit he would not fail.
He knew that a path, though narrow, was a trail
Cut through the obstacles that would lead to the end.

The next step he did to take,
A decision he did not have to make
Because a promise had been made before
For a better road to travel and so much more.

A promise was made that he would not fade,
A promise to all that they would not fall,
Fall from grace as they run the race.
It was on his knees he promised to believe.

It was years, not days, spent in the dessert,
Wandering with not a path to follow.
In the heat, sweat constantly on his brow
He was looking for better, but was never alert.

At the edge of the desert
He looked ahead, not behind,
And saw something that seemed
To be reaching to the heavens above.

It was in seeing that mountain, the majesty of the view,
Feeling the breeze blow through his spirit he knew
That what he had wanted he no longer desired.
He now felt the cooling warmth of a heart afire.

He saw God on that mountain reaching out.
He saw God's glory, saw his glory all about.
He experienced a death and a new birth,
And then he knew his place on this earth.

God rescued a lone figure walking through pain
And promised him a new life forever and beyond.
And that lone figure promised in the rain
To follow the path that led to Jesus and life beyond.

Reflection on The Next Step of Promises

I think that this is the continuation of some of the last few poems. There is nothing that I recall that inspired it other than wanting to write. There is a reason, I just don't know what it is, or don't want to admit it.

Pray Always

I started my day with a prayer
Knowing that I would also receive.
I know that I must always pray for others,
Pray for the needs of my sisters and brothers.

Through my daily prayer I have found
Prayer can be ever mending.
With the many needs that abound
Prayer we should be never ending.

As my thoughts will wander
And my heart does ponder
My first prayer is to Heaven above
That my prayer will reflect his love.

God knows our needs.
Through prayer he feeds
Those in need
As we heed.

We are commanded to pray,
To pray, pray without ceasing.
Asking the Holy Spirit for the words to say
We can experience God's power releasing.

As we feel the release God's power.
Through our prayer we do not cower
As we feel the spirit within us,
The compassion that comes from Jesus.

While praying I know that God is with me
As I go through my day, in all I see.
As I prayed for the needs of another
He has blessed me along with the others.

I am in the presence of God
And as he listens I do too.
As I pray I am blessed by God
As all who pray will be too.

Everyone needs a prayer.
Everyone needs to pray.

Reflection on Pray Always

Again this is not what I thought I would be writing today. It was two nights before this would be posted, Labor Day evening. It wasn't a busy day but is wasn't a wasted day either. I was trying to think about what to write and came up with a couple of ideas. I even had the title of the poem typed on the page. After a minute or so of looking at the titles of the other poems I had written for the book, this poem was written. Again, I asked for help and guidance and got it. Prayer is always there.

Like My Father

Somewhere there are rhymes,
Yes, there have been times,
But I wonder now and then,
I wonder just how and when.

I am my father's son, but am I the one
Who has become more than a son?
Am I him in how I sin
Or am I more than I live for?

No rhymes, well maybe a few,
And today in how I live, in what I do
I have the same addictions to …
He had that led to separation.

I did not grow up with his demons
So what could ever be the reasons
I live in chains and shackles
That keep me from God's love.

He was a man of faith, a man of the church,
Until one day, he no longer prayed.
It was as if there had been a raid
On his soul that destroyed his faith.

No, it wasn't a day, it was years
Of living with the past, constantly with tears.
It was the fear of being unworthy
In the eyes of his wife, his family.
And on his death from too much to drink,
From a death that brought him to the brink
Of eternal, everlasting failure
He prayed and found his treasure.

With our hands clasped together
He knew that from then forever
He would experience the resurrection,
Forgiveness that leads to perfection.

I am my father's son
And what is done is done,
And like my father before me
The grace of God I do see.

Amazing

I heard music with bagpipes and a fife
And knew how wonderful was life,
Amazing grace how sweet the sound.
Standing there I looked around
And it is in that moment I found
The gift from God that was my wife.

Oh, there were years with tears,
Years of hurry and of worry,
Years to forget, of life's regret,
Years of joy starting with a baby boy,
Years of baby girls that maybe,
No, truly brought joy with the baby boy.

Without these years I would have had fears
That being alone would turn me to stone.
I had the love of family because I was me.
I loved them as one because I knew I had won
The battle so many face as they run the race.

The race of today and what may,
What may be, what I may be
As I have confessed I am blessed
By those who love me and what they see
In this lowly man doing what he can
To help them survive and stay alive.

Alive in hope that they may cope
With the world around and its sounds.
And as they cope my prayer for hope,
For all I desire is set on fire
Through the words of Jesus who saves us,

A wretch like me that I may be
A reflection, a connection
To the God of love in Heaven above.

And to help with me, for others to see
He changed my life, he gave me my wife.

Of Truth and Lies

Is it the truth or the lies,
Which one wears the disguise?
There are the hows and the whys
That hide as one of these dies.

Perhaps I have believed
That as I was deceived,
Believed in the message so strong
Never thinking that it could be so wrong.

The sky is blue, this is true.
The earth is round, true it sounds.
Water is wet, though there are those yet
Who do not understand their head is in the sand.

Is it the truth or is it the lies
That in the end will make my heart cry
Because I never tried to know who lied,
Because I do not know how to try?

It is up to me to look beyond the words.
Beyond the one who one or the other does speak,
It is up to me to question what I have heard.
It is the truth, not the lies that I must seek.

Whether the road takes you to the left or the right,
You must never give in without a fight,
A fight within your mind, your soul so that you might
Know the truth when and where it shines its light.

Words That Are Shared

Don't worry, there is no forecast for a snow flurry
And the judge and the jury are no longer in a hurry
To hear another story with details so gory
Yes, I am sorry to have found sentences
For my crime, inserting words that rhyme

Sometimes when exercising the mind
In sorting and cleaning one does find
Thoughts that become words to write
Words in lines that together just might
Be more than one may dare to dream
Words that make the reader want to scream

Either scream with joy or anger
Voices that make the sounds
That express without words
Emotions they have found
From the words of one's thoughts
That others should at all times read

What do you think, what do I think
Do you drink from the glass that I drink
Do your beliefs give you relief
Do my beliefs bring you grief
Or maybe it is the other way
That I grieve at what you say

But we must talk as together we walk
In the life we live, in the love we give
To disagree we must understand
The reasons for another's stand
Just as when we present our side
We must do so not to divide

Respect one another
Our sister and brother
Whether right or wrong
So we may sing a song
Of peace and brotherhood
Of showing each other the good

Pray that we not lead others astray
Pray that there is truth in all we say
Pray that we will find the way
Pray that together we will stay
Pray that the love of God will engulf us all
Pray that this happens before we fall

Before we fall from grace!

Matthew 16:6

I tremble in fear as I write these words,
Not in fear of what the reader may think.
I tremble in fear, in awe of God that stirred
My heart to believe I can be his scribe.

Throughout the Old and New Testaments
There are warnings about false prophets.
Warnings were given during the times of the law
And again today knowing all his people saw.

During the times of the Law
God's chosen ones were instructed
As they sought their release
To eat unleavened bread.

Today we are saved by unleavened bread,
Jesus the bread of life knew no sin.

In Matthew we find that the rulers of the law,
The Pharisees and the Sadducees, fought what they saw.
Though seeing they were unbelieving,
Missing God's mighty wonder and awe.

After refusing the demands of those who were blind
Jesus left the religious leaders and others behind.
When they went across the lake,
the disciples forgot to take bread.
"Be careful," Jesus said to them.
"Be on your guard against the yeast
of the Pharisees and Sadducees."
Matthew 16:5,6

The disciples perhaps confused,
Or perhaps like a writer confounded,
Wondered if what he said
Was because they didn't bring any bread.

Knowing of their discussion, Jesus asked,
*"You of little faith, why are you talking
among yourselves about having no bread?*
(Matthew 16:8)

And he reminded them of the times
They gathered baskets and baskets of loaves
That were left over, which were more,
More than they had when they began.

Jesus continued,
*"How is it you don't understand that I
was not talking to you about bread?
Be on guard against the yeast
of the Pharisees and Sadducees."
Matthew 16:11*

Then the disciples knew as we should know
That it was not the yeast used in the bread
That they should guard against, but the preaching
Of those leaders in power and their false teaching.

Today there are those who profess
To know better than the rest,
That the Jesus they teach
They will show you how to reach.

God's ways are not our ways
And any word we add or change
That leads one in need astray,
For us life will become stranger,
Stranger with danger.

Jesus, the Bread of Life, needs no yeast.
Nothing needs to be added, no nothing,
How do we improve on perfection,
Ours through his death and resurrection?

We need to read God's word,
We need to pray for wisdom
To know that the words of man we have heard
Are the words that rule God's Kingdom.

The Wonder of God's Way

God's love is shown and Jesus is known
As the words of King David are heard
Many years after and many years before,
After the creation and before the resurrection.

In times of grace and in time of waste
God's love for us never falters, never fails.
His is a love we may never understand,
While on this earth we are merely man.

David writes:
the LORD is compassionate and gracious,
slow to anger; abounding in love.
He will not always accuse,
nor will he harbor his anger forever;
he does not treat us as our sins deserve
or repay us according to our iniquities.
For as high as the heavens are above the earth,
so great is his love for those who fear him;
as far as the east is from the west,
so far has he removed our transgressions from us.
Psalm 103:7-12

How can we on this earth understand this love?
We live our lives struggling for love
While we struggle at times to give our love.
We shake our neighbor's hands with winter gloves.

If we have fear for the Lord, the awe and respect he deserves,
We have opened the door to our hearts to receive his grace,
If we truly believe and accept this and are not reserved
In our faith, he is faithful to forgive and remember never.

Be thankful that as Isaiah writes of God,
For my thoughts are not your thoughts,
neither are your ways my ways."
declares the LORD .
As the heavens are higher than the earth,
so are my ways higher than your ways
and my thoughts than your thoughts.
Isaiah 55:8,9

Live in awe filled wonder and his voice will not thunder
Because of who he is, as we live, he forgives.
By faith through his grace, we have the gift to forever live
Through the death of his Son, who took upon himself our sin.

Be thankful God is who he is and always will be,
Be thankful God loves you and loves me,
Be thankful God created us in love
So by believing we will see him in heaven above.

God so loves us that he sent his only Son to die for our transgressions.
If his ways were our ways, we would still be dying in those transgressions.
Be thankful and accept his love, the gift of his son
So one day you will be with him when with this world you are done.

Chapter 5, Drawing on Her Inspiration

Introduction - Tim

In March of this year I attended a John Courtney Newman talk with my wife at St. Stephen Church. While enjoying refreshments during the break I was talking to Gwen's mother, Christine. We talked about a book someone we both knew had written. Christine told me about her daughter, Gwen, and the artwork she has done. She told me about some drawings she had done during a youth group retreat at St. Stephen's. This led to me telling her about a book my seven year old grandson Eli and I had put together for Christmas last year. Eli drew pictures of winter scenes and Christmas and I wrote a poem for each of them. I asked if I could see the drawings and maybe I could write a poem for each drawing and we could put something together like Eli and I did.

I must say that I found the drawings inspiring. The thoughts expressed and the drawings spoke to me. I was impressed that someone Gwen's age had such deep faith. It gives me hope.

I have been blessed to be part of this endeavor. Gwen's inspiration is truly inspiring.

Tim Carter
May 21, 2017

Hello Readers

First, I would like to say that I am thrilled that this collection of artwork and poetry has crossed your path, and I hope that in reading it, you will find a little more enjoyment in your life today. Second, I would like to say a HUGE thank you to Tim Carter for making this possible and for feeling inspired enough by my drawings to create such beautiful works of poetry.

As for myself, I am a firm believer that inspiration comes in many forms. I am not really certain why my hand and brain connected that day to create these pictures. I was at a Women's retreat at my church, and I remember feeling myself start to zone out, and lose focus in the message. I just recall looking up at the Crucifix, that is positioned at the front of the church. That one glance at the church's traditional representation of the Lord, and I knew that HE was in the room with us. Not just in the room- but in my heart. I turned over one of the pages I had been given for the retreat, and began to draw.

Now, I have only ever taken one art class and am not very good at drawing, but the pictures I drew that day came straight from a place of spiritual influence. Once I started, I could not stop thinking about new messages that I wanted to convey through the imagery. Too often, the Lord's Word gets lost in all of the fancy liturgical jargon, to kids of the coming generation. Visuals are the most effective way to convey messages, and I believe that is why God put the thought in my mind, to spread some scripture in a way that could reach the most people.

In summary, love and a firm trust in God's plans for me were my inspiration behind these pieces. On behalf of myself and Tim Carter, I hope you thoroughly enjoy this book as much as we did creating it for you!

God Bless,
Gwen Allen

A Soldier for the Lord

There is more than the battle to be won
There is more that we are here for.
If we are to follow God's Son
We do not fight as if it's a war.

No, our mission is to share his love.
If we love God, we are commanded to love others.

Maybe the battle rages within us.
If we are one with Jesus,
The battle has been won.
We are raised with his Son.

If God is in us, his love we must share.
Through our sharing we show we care,
Not just for others, but for the Father
Who loves us in spite of ourselves.

We must show the love in our heart,
Love that is for all to see.
As the sun rises our days start.
Is love what our day will be?

Love will overcome hate.
If we do not show His love,
What will be the fate
Of those we overlook?

A soldier, marching forward,
Sharing God's loving word,
Showing his saving grace
To a stranger's face.

If we are to stand,
We must follow his command.

1 John 1:1 – 5:21

Be a Soldier Unto the Lord

In this earthly world we live in,
Where some take and others give,
Where one can believe
Or one can deceive,
Where love can prevail
If we do not fail.

A soldier unto the Lord –
First we must believe
So love will prevail.

It's not a neighbor,
Nor is it a friend,
No, not in the end.
It's not man,
Though many times
We think he can
Be the reason.
But since the fall,
When we heed his call,
We are in the season
To guard his rhymes.

One by one
As followers
Of his Son
We are attacked
Not by man,

But rather by
Rulers
And authorities,
Powers of a
Dark world
And
Spiritual forces
In the
Heavenly realms.

So we become a soldier,
A soldier for the Lord.
We put on the armor of God
To protect against the evil horde.

The belt of truth around our waist,
The truth we receive from Jesus.
The breastplate of righteousness,
Protected by his sacrifice.
Feet fitted with readiness,
The peace of his word within us.
Then taking up the shield of faith,
To extinguish the flaming arrows.
And the helmet of salvation
So all may see who stands with us.

And as we prepare
We must pray
Each and every day
That we care,

That we, one by one,
Showing God's love,
Sharing the way
Tomorrow and today.

We may be a soldier for the Lord,
Not in sowing seeds of discord,
But seeds of love, truth and salvation
And eternal redemption.

Ephesians 6

The Reflection

Beauty is in the eye of the beholder
and beauty is what is beholden.
God saw the beauty of Mary,
a beauty of motherhood for his Son,
And he saw the beauty of his Son,
in the sacrifice for those he loved.
That beauty God shares with the girl
as she walks through this world.

As she gazes at the reflection
she sees the love God has for her.
It is this love that she sees taking her hands
and guiding her through her life.

It is a love of trust,
something she must
receive and give
in the life she lives.

What reflection do you see
when looking in the mirror?

Protected Forever and Ever

The rain falls from the sky.
Some days we wonder why
No matter how we try
We cannot help but cry.

Yes, the world rains down
With trials and tribulations,
As we are thinking we may drown
In the sorrows of temptation.

Let us not worry and fret.
A prayer has been said,
The way He has led,
The path He has set.

Before the cross came a prayer.
"While I have been with them,
I protected them and kept the safe
by that name you gave me." John 17:12\

Then He died for our sins
Knowing we would stray.
The rain would pour down,
Our faith washed away.

Even in those moments, if we do believe,
Because of His love we need never grieve.
Through His death and resurrection
We have eternal His protection.

Yes, even those moments
We lose sight of our faith's face,
By the words of our faith
We are saved by God's grace.

Believe,
Accept,
Profess
Jesus, the King whose reign
Protects us in our weakness.

Our faith may fail,
But He never will.

Mary and Joseph had the first UNPLANNED PREGNANCY. Their child was born, and became the LIGHT of the World.
When you choose abortion, you are blowing out a LIGHT the WORLD so desperately NEEDS.

An Unplanned Pregnancy

"Mary and Joseph had the first unplanned pregnancy." (from the drawing")

She might have asked,
"What if Jesus had been aborted?"
But she didn't, I did.
It was this birth that lead to a death
That lead to our rebirth, if we believe.

Jesus, born as a human,
In the flesh as man.
But a part of him still God.
Maybe to us that is odd.
But we . . .
Only by faith can understand.

How many candles in the Bible did God light?
In our times of need where would we be,
If candles had been blown out?
What if Abraham,
What if Noah,
What if David or Solomon,
What if the Prophets,
What if Moses,
What if the Apostles.
What if Paul,
. . .
What if your parents,
What if you,
What would the world have missed,
What blessings denied,
And tomorrow

What will we never know
Without an eternal candle.

With every life we destroy
We destroy a part of His Paternity.
There is one less child who will enjoy
Being His child for eternity.

Yes, we are children of God
So we must help those in need.
As his children his command we must heed,
To love one another as Jesus has loved us.

Pray
Love
Help

Whichever way the Wind Will Blow... Only God Can Weather the Storm.

Whichever Way the Wind Will Blow

A storm, a boat, the disciples with Jesus . . .
He got up, rebuked the wind and said to the waves,
"Quiet! Be Still!" Then the wind died down
And it was completely calm. Mark 4:39

When there is a gentle breeze
Then we find a life of ease,
But when the wind will blow
Does our spirit sink low?

It is at those times
When facing life's storms,
With the wind at our face
As we run our life's race,
We feel tattered and torn,
We lose track of His rhyme.

It in these times of trial
We must remember our faith.
When the acrid taste of bile
Rises we must remember our place.

God is on our side,
So we never need to hide.
We have His gentle breath
On which we can rest.

The Holy Spirit moves
As a gentle breeze,
Calming the winds,
Restoring our faith.
It is the breath of God,

It is His Word at creation
That calms the storms
Yesterday,
Today and
Tomorrow.

We just have to believe.
Ask, pray and we shall receive.

With God we can weather the storm.

Chapter Six,
The End of the Story

A September to Remember

Yes, the days are over
You can smell the clover
Kids are playing a game
Red rover, red rover
Send anybody over

Maybe it's not the same
It seems like a hundred years ago
Or maybe less as one does grow
It seems that time ages
As we grow older
Maybe a little bolder
As we earned our wages

I read a poem by someone I knew
I met on a trip in the morning dew
The words scattered on the page
Were meant for me to engage
In thoughtful reflection
Not in the mirror
But in my soul

Words unlike mine
Seemed to be a sign
That what I would find
And what I left behind
Were never the same
Not by any kind of name

The days to write
Were to be passed on
So someone else might

Continue the fight
Before I passed on
Before my words ended
No longer defended

This is just about the words
I hope you have heard
As in your mind you read
Not pondering the meaning
But knowing somewhere instead
They were meant for redeeming

The book is complete
Not a human feat
But by the word
Of a voice I heard

Concluding Prayer

Dear Father in Heaven,
It is not just what you have done,
But what you do every day
Yesterday, today and tomorrow.

Lord, I know that in prayer
The words need not rhyme.
You are the rhyme and in me
You have blessed me with your words.

I may not always know what to say,
But I know when I take time to pray
Your Holy Spirit living within me will lead the way
So that through my prayer I will not be led astray.

I thank you Father for my salvation
I thank you for loving me so much
That you sent your Son to die for my sins.
For that I do not know what to say, . . . I love you.

You have taken this wretch of a man
And lifted him up so he may see
All that in you, he can be.
I pray that your presence will never leave.

No, it is not you who will leave.
I pray that it is not me.
Dear Lord, I pray that your word,
The rhymes you have for us,
Will shake this world with your love
So that one day we will all not just see,
But be in Heaven above.

Save us from ourselves.
Take us off the shelves
Where we collect only dust.
Through your Son, Jesus,
I pray that all believe
And receive your grace.

Amen and Amen

Also by Tim Carter – *God's Rhyme*

Read about the beginning of the journey from love through birthright, the carpenter's son, somehow, God's rhyme, the every man, touching the heart of God, sixteen days in Hunter's house.

You are love
and how I love you,
you, Jesus are love I can be.
Rejected by most
in his short human life.
He has created
in each of us
by the nails.
He understood
that when a mother
loves an alcoholic
you pray.
She's always had your heart,
She always will, your little girl.
The simple oddity of life
is God's rhyme.
He needs us as much as we need him,
by reaching out he makes us stronger.
The awesome privilege by helping the orphan .. ,
of touching, yes touching, the heart of God.
You who are weary from the day's race,
Come and rest in his amazing grace.

Also by Tim Carter – *God Still Rhymes*

Read about the clock on the wall, the first valentine, the day before his wedding, lost in prayer, the trees and the crashing waves, the joy of sadness, the science of prayer and God's grace.

For it is in God our hours
are measured,
All your giving
is what you are living,
the hours go by
so slowly
between the times
I see you.
Lustful
for my answer
came another.
Sin started with the fruit of a tree
and ended with the death on a tree.
Like waves crashing upon a barren shore
your love so overwhelms me.
On this Easter day
he was able to turn
our Sorrow into Joy.
A doctor received part of the miracle
that through prayer everyone did seek.
We can say it and we can believe
we are saved by grace,
our lives he has repaired
so what he has prepared,
the works for us to do,
we help more than a few.

www.ingramcontent.com/pod-product-compliance
Lightning Source LLC
Chambersburg PA
CBHW071326110526
44591CB00010B/1043